Managing Politics and Conflict in Projects

Managing Politics and Conflict in Projects

BRIAN IRWIN, PMP

MANAGEMENTCONCEPTS

MANAGEMENT CONCEPTS

8230 Leesburg Pike, Suite 800
Vienna, VA 22182
(703) 790-9595
Fax: (703) 790-1371
www.managementconcepts.com

Printed in the United States of America
10 9 8 7 6 5 4 3 2 1

Library of Congress Cataloging-in-Publication Data

Irwin, Brian.
 Managing politics and conflict in projects / Brian Irwin.
   p. cm.
 ISBN 978-1-56726-221-6
 1. Management—Study and teaching. I. Title.
HD30.4.I78 2008
658.4'04—dc22

                                             2007031248

About the Author

Brian Irwin, MSM, PMP, has more than 15 years of project experience in diverse industries including personal computers, engineering, information technology, aerospace, and defense. He is currently the president of PM Team Dynamics (www.pmteamdynamics.com), a project management consulting firm specializing in project audits, troubled project assessment and recovery, and project startup facilitation.

Mr. Irwin formerly worked for Hewlett Packard in Fort Collins, Colorado, where he tested midrange LINUX and UNIX-based servers. He previously worked for Gateway Computers, where he experienced the fast-paced environment of a company growing at a monthly rate approaching 100 percent. Mr. Irwin has also worked as an associate member of the professional staff at The Johns Hopkins University Applied Physics Laboratory in Laurel, Maryland, where he tested infrared seekers for the U.S. Navy's ballistic missile defense program.

Mr. Irwin, a certified project management professional, holds a Bachelor of Science in Electrical Engineering and a Master of Science in Management with a specialization in Project Management from Colorado Technical University in Colorado Springs, Colorado.

*This book is dedicated to the memory of
my loving mother*

Caroline R. Irwin

The guidance and love she so willingly supplied
during my youth is what provided me
the discipline and motivation to complete
a graduate-level education and, ultimately, this work.
I feel her loss every day but the confidence
and inspiration she instilled remains with me.

Contents

Forewords. xiii

Preface xvii

Acknowledgments xxi

CHAPTERS

1   **Understanding the Project Environment** 1

The Art and Science of Project Management. 1

Challenges in the Project Environment. 3

Lessons Learned 11

Key Points 12

Take Action 12

2   **Politics: Project Management Fact-of-Life** 21

Politics: The Necessary and Vital Project Skill. 22

Project Management: A Political Art 24

Politics and the Project Lifecycle 25

Organizational Culture 30

Project Politics and Self-Awareness 34

Key Points 36

Take Action 37

3 Conflict: Don't Fear the Inevitable 45
The Necessity of Project Conflict 46
Source of Conflict in Project Process Groups 47
Types of Conflict 52
Conflict Resolution Modes 54
Generational Differences 57
Key Points 59
Take Action 60

4 Project Stakeholders 69
The Stakeholder Management Process 70
Mapping Stakeholders 78
Key Points 80
Take Action 80

5 Communication 89
Communication Modes 90
Barriers to Communication 93
The Path to Effective Communication 97
Key Points 102
Take Action 102

6 Negotiation 111
The Need to Negotiate 112
Negotiation Considerations 114
Preparing for Negotiations 115
Active Listening and Negotiation 117
Emotions and Conflict in Negotiations 118
Key Points 120
Take Action 121

7 **Multidirectional Relationship Management** 133
Lateral Relationships with Peers and Colleagues . . . 135
Upward Relationships with Your Boss 137
Upward Relationships with Executives 139
Downward Relationships with the Project Team . . . 140
Key Points 142
Take Action 143

8 **Devising a Political Strategy** 151
Observe and Plan 152
Take Action 155
Take Time to Reflect 158
Key Points 159
Take Action 160

9 **The Leadership Element** 167
Traits of Effective Leadership 168
The DTAB Project Leadership Model. 176
Key Points 179
Take Action 180

10 **Implications** 185
Create a Positive Project Culture 185
Acknowledge the Existence of Politics
    and Conflict 186
Don't Forget Humor. 187

APPENDIXES

A **Organizational Structures** 193
Functional Organizational Structure. 193
Matrix Organizational Structure 196
Projectized Organizational Structure 199

B **Political Savvy Quiz Answers**. 203
Political Savvy Individuals. 203
The Results 206

Index 209

Forewords

Early in my project management career, I believed that my good work would speak for itself. I was a good project manager and delivered my projects on time, within budget, and consistent with quality standards. But year after year I watched as other people were promoted ahead of me. I always felt like I was missing some trick-of-the-trade or some type of connection that would make me stand out among others.

After years of experience, I finally realized that I had to manage the *political* work environment to really succeed, and after implementing the lessons I learned, I was finally promoted to a higher project management position.

I've since become a project management instructor and consultant, and the number of questions my students and others pose about political issues is striking. The politics of project management—conflicts with colleagues, communication problems, and so on—is just as important to them as the actual mechanics of project management. I'm always looking for resources that can help me train project managers to identify and respond to political issues.

Managing Politics and Conflict in Projects is just the type of resource I've been looking for to help my students and clients negotiate their political environment. The book's conversational, yet no-nonsense style walks you step-by-step through the "soft" issues of project management, including written, oral, and nonverbal communications, and negotiating and influencing skills. It offers tips for managing stakeholder and sponsor expectations, resolving conflict, and preventing conflict when possible. *Managing Politics and Conflict in Projects* covers each of these topics and more, with an emphasis on the perspectives of project managers and leaders dealing with political issues in a project environment.

What I love about this book is that it's not limited to specific industries or professions. Project managers across all industries, regardless of individual experience or status, need these soft skills to succeed. *Managing Politics and Conflict in Projects* offers a wealth of information that will provide readers the information they need to advance to the next level as project managers.

> *Claudia M. Baca*, PMP
> President, Claudia M. Baca Project Management
>   Consulting Services
> PMI Certified *OPM3*® Assessor, consultant,
>   and best-selling author

☐

Managing Politics and Conflict in Projects is an interesting and insightful contribution to the project management literature. As project professionals, we hope never to encounter conflict, and we hope we won't need to engage too often in politics. But politics and conflict are inevitably part of any project environment, and unfortunately, there are few resources to guide us.

In an easy-to-read fashion, Brian Irwin has written a book that shows readers how to move up the career ladder by effectively navigating and utilizing politics and conflict for project, team, and organizational success. *Managing Politics and Conflict in Projects* is essentially an amalgamation of Mr. Irwin's valuable, professional lessons learned, gained during his diverse career as a project manager.

Managing Politics and Conflict in Projects shows readers how project management techniques can benefit from improvements in soft skills. In the chapter on stakeholders, for example, Mr. Irwin describes a process that project teams can follow to address stakeholder strengths and weaknesses, craft a plan to manage these stakeholders according to those characteristics, and follow through with stakeholders as appropriate. By taking time to be cognizant of stakeholder characteristics and status, project managers can more appropriately and more effectively control important expectations and relationships.

In another important chapter on leadership, Mr. Irwin discusses how important it is for project managers to develop their leadership skills as facilitators and mentors, suggesting a collaborative approach that emphasizes honesty, self-reflection, and open dialog. *Managing Politics and Conflict in Projects* shows project managers how to become the type of team member they would themselves like to lead.

The use of key review points, tips, actions, and a fictional case study woven throughout the entire book all combine to make *Managing Politics and Conflict in Projects* an excellent resource not only for project managers, but for anyone seeking valuable information emphasizing leadership, interpersonal skills, and communications skills.

Ginger Levin, DPA, CAPM, PMP, PgMP
PMI Certified *OPM3*® Assessor and consultant

☐

Preface

Why a book on politics and conflict in project management? Simply, because I sincerely believe in the ability of many project managers to deal more effectively with complex organizational and interpersonal situations. As organizations increasingly adopt the practice of project management to achieve their goals, more and more individuals are thrust into project leadership positions without adequate training. In particular, many project managers aren't adept in the soft skills, political savvy, and conflict management skills that are vital to project success.

A recent Internet search on "project management education" revealed the great breadth of possibilities for individuals seeking to learn project management skills. Indeed, the majority of project managers today are well-versed in the techniques of scheduling, cost estimating, and other useful and necessary project management "hard" skills.

However, project success also relies directly on the ability of project managers to use soft skills to communicate, negotiate, and influence within a project environment that inevitably involves politics and conflict. Understanding organizational politics and conflict is necessary to thrive as a project manager.

If you work in a project-driven organization and are wondering whether you might have something to gain from this book, ask yourself these questions:

- *Are you held accountable for leading projects to successful completion but get frustrated because you are not given the authority to make decisions and take action that would ensure project success?*

- *Do you consider it unethical to engage in organizational politics?*

- *Have you been in confrontations with colleagues about project team assignments and the roles of project team members?*

- *Do you view conflict as unproductive?*

- *Does your stomach sometimes knot up at the thought of bringing up a difficult topic in a team meeting or executive briefing?*

- *Have you cringed at the thought of dealing with a difficult coworker, especially if they have more positional power than you?*

- *Have you ever found yourself in the trying situation of negotiating for resources from a colleague with whom you have a strained relationship?*

If you answered "yes" to any of these questions, *Managing Politics and Conflict in Projects* offers information that can be of immediate use to you on your projects. While any member of a project team can benefit from a greater awareness of the topics discussed in this book, project managers, project sponsors, and executives within project-driven organizations will find the information especially relevant.

Why I Chose to Write This Book

When I began my career as an electrical engineer, I had no clear understanding of the impact organizational politics and conflict would have on the achievement of my professional goals. As far as I was concerned, to advance my career, it was important for me to simply be the best engineer possible.

While it is true that being skilled in what you do is—and should be—a requisite to promotion, it is not enough. Having a firm grasp of an organization's political climate and culture is crucial to ascend the corporate ladder to positions in leadership and upper management.

It is common to consider conflict as inherently bad and political play as an underhanded tactic of corporate bullies. It's natural to want to avoid conflict and to seek a level of equilibrium among individuals, especially among members of your project team. But I've realized over time that conflict is absolutely necessary in projects, and that political play can be used wisely to advance everyone's goals.

Organization of the Book

Managing Politics and Conflict in Projects is organized into ten chapters, each about a different dynamic related to politics and conflict in project environments. The chapters were written so each can be read independently as needed.

Key points are summarized at the end of each chapter, along with a list of topic-related techniques you can put to immediate use. Additional tips highlighted throughout the text provide practical advice. Finally, a running fictional case study at the end of each chapter illustrates the application of the chapter topic. The case study should be read sequentially by chapter, as its content builds upon previous chapters.

I hope you enjoy the book and I wish you the best of luck on future projects!

Brian Irwin
Cedar Rapids, Iowa

☐

Acknowledgments

Writing this book has been on my mind for several years now and represents years of experiences and observations in projects ranging from the development of small-scale software to the development of new, complex systems. The final product would not have been possible without the extraordinary efforts of many who were either directly or indirectly involved.

Through this journey, my wife Lynn has been there to provide encouragement. She has suffered through many evenings of me not being by her side at night while I conducted research and completed the manuscript. My children have sacrificed play time so that daddy could *work on his book*. For my wife and two sons, Garrett and Shane, I am forever thankful and indebted for your love and support. You three very special people are my joy in life.

I'd also like to thank the entire team at Management Concepts—Myra Strauss and Courtney Chiaparas in particular. Myra Strauss was an ever-forgiving and understanding person when I would call to ask for just a little more time to complete the manuscript. I thank you all for providing me with an opportunity to realize my dream of being a published author. You saw the desire I carry inside of me and gave me the chance. Thank you!

I would also like to thank those I sent the manuscript to for review, quotations, and much needed feedback (although it was sometimes hard to listen to). For your honesty and openness, I thank you. In particular, I'd like to thank Claudia Baca and Ginger Levin for reviewing the manuscript and writing their forewords. Claudia is truly a professional project manager in every respect, and she has always made herself available as a mentor, role model, and friend. Thank you very much, Claudia, for all you have given me. Ginger Levin has proven to be a very warm and open individual whose work during her illustrious career in project management has inspired me. She's an accomplished author and I've come to learn very much from her writing.

Ramesh Kandadai is an outstanding project manager, mentor, and friend. Ramesh has helped me through several of my endeavors and continues to provide the type of support, encouragement, and honest feedback that all professional project managers require. I look forward to a long personal and professional friendship, and I hope that he is getting as much out of our relationship as I am. Thank you, Ramesh.

To Wes Chitwood, Darrell Kern, and Art Cohan—you know why I'm thanking you and the special bond we share. You are a source of strength for me when things get tough. The answer is in the rock.

Finally, I want to thank my father, Harry Irwin. A stronger man I've never met. He is a World War II veteran, a hard-working role model to his four sons, and my hero. To my dad, thank you for all of your support and attention during my years at home. You and mom made it a great place to grow up. With any luck and a lot of hard work, I can provide the same good example for my family that you set for me during my youth.

☐

Understanding the Project Environment

To understand the unique challenges inherent in project management, we must first understand the environment in which it takes place. This opening chapter reviews the characteristics of the project management environment and examines some of the challenges it presents. It also introduces some of the complexities related to managing projects in a global business environment.

The Art and Science of Project Management

The *PMBOK® Guide* defines three distinct characteristics of a project.[1] First, a project is temporary. In contrast to an ongoing operation, a project has a distinct beginning and a distinct end. Second, a project is unique. Its purpose is to create a product, service, or other specific result. Finally, because it is temporary and unique, a project is progressively elaborated—or iteratively refined—until the solution reaches a sufficient level of definition or completeness.

An organization that attempts to undertake projects reaching across functional, cultural, and business boundaries should expect to encounter struggles and complexities. The deciding factor in a project's success will be how the project manager responds to these challenges.

Crafting a project charter, assembling project schedules, analyzing variances to cost and schedule, and developing risk management plans are all part of the *science* of project management. Negotiating for project resources (financial and personnel), influencing key stakeholders, and leading the team—those are part of the *art* of project management. Art and science together define the skill of the successful project manager. Neither can exist without the other if there is to be a successful outcome.

Usually, it's not the initiating, planning, executing, controlling, and closing—the science of project management—that causes migraines and heartburn for project managers; rather, it's the need for constant communication, negotiation, political play, and influence. These skills must be applied in a multidirectional manner—downward to the project manager's team, upward to the project sponsors, sideways to peers and colleagues, inward to themselves, and outward to external suppliers and partners. The project manager must also keep focused on corporate strategy (forward) and how his or her project fits into it, while simultaneously monitoring and controlling the performance and execution of the project (backward). Figure 1-1 illustrates this concept graphically.

FIGURE 1-1 The Art of Influence through Relationships in Project Management

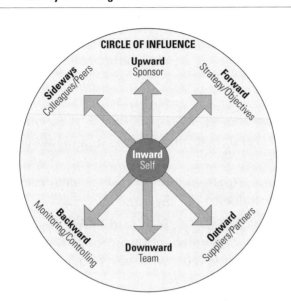

Challenges in the Project Environment

The project environment offers many challenges for even the most experienced project manager. Four key challenges common to every project environment include: communication, competition for scarce resources, unclear project goals, and lack of power. In recent years, increasing project globalization has presented an additional challenge to project managers around the world.

Communication

Project managers could just as well be titled "project communicators" because they must keep all the project stakeholders

TIP: Provide a weekly status to the project sponsor even if it hasn't been asked for. This will give you an opportunity to build a relationship and serve to keep your sponsor actively engaged in the project.

engaged and informed during the entire project lifecycle. As a project manager, you can expect to spend up to 90 percent of your time communicating with stakeholders— sponsors, team members, resource managers, vendors, and partners, to name just a few. (In Chapter 4 we'll take a closer look at stakeholders and their specific interests and influences.)

What makes project communication so challenging? First, not all stakeholders need the same information. Second, not all stakeholders need, or want, the communication to be in the same medium (e.g., email, phone, meetings, presentations). The message will also differ with the type of information being communicated (e.g., status reports, schedule changes, scope changes, meeting minutes), as well as the frequency of those communications.

Competition for Scarce Resources

Competition for valuable and scarce resources is another challenge for the project manager. Effectively dealing with this challenge requires that you understand the technical skills critical to each task within your project and that you effectively negotiate with resource managers to have the appropriate person(s) assigned to those tasks.

In many industries, especially in information technology (IT), portfolio management is becoming a popular way to deal with these issues. Portfolio management enables an organization to apply its resources across the board to all of its programs and projects in ways that optimize their use.

Portfolio Management

The Project Management Institute (PMI) defines portfolio management as "a collection of projects (temporary endeavors undertaken to create a unique product, service, or result) and/or programs (a group of related projects managed in a coordinated way to obtain benefits and control not available from managing them individually) and other work that are grouped together to facilitate the effective management of that work to meet strategic business objectives."[2] In other words, portfolio management helps organizations ensure that valuable resources are effectively prioritized across several endeavors.

Political savvy is very important to project managers working in a portfolio management environment. Consider the project manager working on one of the low-priority projects in the portfolio. He or she may continuously struggle to keep resources as the needs of high-priority projects shift.

Unclear Project Goals

If you do not know where you are going, you will not know when you get there. Many projects are challenged from the beginning because the sponsor has not provided clear objectives and well-defined goals. What does success look like to the project's sponsor, its customer, and members of your project team? What are the goals of the project?

The Project Management Institute's *PMBOK® Guide* describes projects as *temporary* and *unique*.[3] That means there must be a specific reason for the project and there must be a distinct beginning and end to the work. But in many instances, the project manager will be handed a project without a clear definition of its scope, even though the project schedule and budget have both been set. Virtually every project manager can identify with the scenario of having a mandated budget and schedule. How can you possibly manage to a dictated schedule and budget without a solid definition of the project's ultimate goal?

By working to define the goals of the project, you can help the project sponsor define the project's scope and outcome. Keep in mind that as the project manager, your job is to communicate the work that can be done within the bounds of the directed schedule and budget. If you do not, you've essentially accepted the task as directed and have set your project up for failure prior to kickoff. In today's business environment, cost and schedule are paramount for corporate executives. As companies strive to beat the competition to market, deadlines for development and testing are shrinking and budgets are being cut to increase profit margins.

It's easy to see why a project manager must have well-honed interpersonal skills. It's not easy—without jeopardizing your career—to communicate the impacts of unrealistic project schedules and budgets to corporate executives, who are in turn under immense pressure from shareholders and corporate boards. To be successful, the project manager must understand the political environment of the organization and how to communicate effectively at all of its levels.

Lack of Power

In many organizations, the project manager operates without formal positional power over project team members. Team members may be connected to a project manager on paper, but still report to a functional manager who is responsible for their performance reviews and raises. This creates a situation that can easily lead to conflict and struggle. The project manager is placed in a position of assigning project tasks to team members who do not report to him or her.

Figure 1-2 provides a summary of the three major types of organizational structures. Refer to Appendix A for a detailed discussion of each organizational structure, including the advantages and disadvantages of each.

If departmental goals are in conflict with the project, a team member's priority may be to align with the situation of the

FIGURE 1-2 Three Major Organizational Structures

Organizational Structure	Team Members Report to	Project Manager Authority	Note
Functional	Functional Manager	Low	In a functional organizational structure, the project manager and functional manager roles are synonymous.
Matrix	Functional Manager	Mid	Matrix organizations provide limited power to the project manager. Team members report to a personnel (functional) manager, who performs performance appraisals and yearly salary increases. Team members in a matrix organization may be torn between project and departmental priorities, which can affect project performance.
Projectized	Project Manager	High	Projectized structures provide the most power to project managers. In this type of structure all personnel report directly to the project manager. However, near the end of the project, team members may become anxious if no follow-on project work is scheduled, because their job security diminishes if they don't have a project to work on.

TIP: Offer to provide performance feedback to the functional manager of project team members. Doing so will allow you to leverage some of the functional manager's formal authority over team members performing your project tasks.

moment, which may not be that of the project. For example, consider a matrix organization in which team members report to a functional manager but are assigned to projects individually. These team members may have goals that are aligned with their functional manager's goals instead of their project manager's goals.

Alternatively, consider a projectized organization, in which the team member is assigned to, and reports to, the project manager full-time. The goals of the team member will most definitely map to the project's goals. Formal power is much more apparent in the projectized structure than it is in the matrix structure.

The project manager must be in constant communication with resource managers to understand where their project falls on the priority scale, because resource managers assign personnel and other resources to their projects. If you sense your project is not a high priority on the resource manager's list, consider this a risk to your project, proactively manage it, and make contingency plans. If appropriate, elevate the situation to the project sponsor for assistance and guidance.

Project Globalization

Spurred by new technology, corporate mergers and acquisitions, and international joint ventures, business is becoming more global in nature. The globalization of business is in turn leading to the globalization of project management. For the project manager, an international project adds another level of complexity on top of an already complex project environment and necessitates increased cultural and interpersonal awareness.

Project managers should consider several factors when undertaking a global project. The first requisite is to understand the culture of the country (or countries) in which your project is undertaken. This is of vital importance because, for example, courtesies extended in one culture may be viewed as insults in another. Effective project management—both domestically and internationally—of course requires that you not insult your partners, suppliers, customers, subcontractors, or sponsors. But the chance for a misstep is much greater when you're dealing with stakeholders from other countries and cultures.

TIP: One of the best non-technical global management books I've found to help understand the protocols and negotiating strategies of other countries is *Kiss, Bow, or Shake Hands*, by Terri Morrison and Wayne A. Conway.[4] This handy book tests your cultural IQ for each country and provides you with a historical overview, a synopsis of the type of government, and some important things to know before you travel to that country.

As an international project manager you may not have enough control, even with the backing of your corporate executives. This is especially true if you are leading a project that requires collaboration with other companies. Your organization may be tasked with leading the project as the prime contractor, but other contractors may hinder your success. This sort of problem can occur in domestic projects, of course, but it can be particularly difficult if you're working with foreign companies.

You may also have to take into consideration local and international regulations and restrictions. Be sure to address them early on, in the project planning phase. Also plan to allocate additional schedule and budget management reserves to

TIP: While it's important for every project to have an executive sponsor, it's absolutely critical that an international project have a strong one. As the project manager, you will need to work hand-in-hand with your sponsor throughout the course of your international project to elicit the appropriate level of negotiation, authorization, and support required to drive a successful outcome. In my experience with international projects, I've often found it necessary to communicate with my sponsor on a weekly basis. Work to ensure that your sponsor stays engaged and informed.

allow for unforeseen problems related to international regulatory requirements.

Logistical issues, like time zone differences, can also be problematic. I once worked on an international project that had the core team located in the U.S. midwest, a partner contractor on the west coast, other project team members in the United Kingdom, and the customer in Asia. Needless to say, many project meetings occurred during the midnight hour, causing fatigue and, in some instances, an attention-to-detail deficit.

Another logistical problem is dealing with differing currencies. This should be considered when performing budget variance analysis, discussing prices with the customer (exchange rates change daily), and estimating travel costs.

One final logistical item to be aware of is international holidays. Be sure to consider international holidays when planning your projects to avoid setting meetings during inappropriate times.

You should also understand the increased visibility of an international project to the outside world. Because they are usually greater in size and scope, international projects tend to draw more attention than domestic projects from stakeholders and occasionally, from external parties like political groups and press. Because of this increased interest, the price of failure may be magnified.

There are many other ways in which international projects increase the complexity of the project environment; approaching international projects just like another domestic project is a recipe for disaster. If the project manager works with team members without paying attention to cultural differences and other factors, the project has an increased chance for failure.

Another area of risk in an international project is lack of measurement during the project execution phase. While performance measurement is important on all projects, it's critical to the health of a global project. The project manager must make measuring the project a priority. To give an analogy: If it's possible to cover the distance of one mile on a domestic project before measuring baseline performance against the plan, you should move only 500 feet before assessing progress in an international project. Taking the pulse of an international project frequently is a necessity. Avoid the temptation to treat the project just like it's a domestic one.

> **TIP:** Measure performance against the baseline plan on an international project more frequently (at least twice as often) than on a domestic project. Your chances of identifying cost, schedule, and quality problems early in the project lifecycle will increase, thereby allowing you to implement corrective action before it's too late.

Lessons Learned

It is a good idea to gather lessons learned as projects—both domestic and international—progress. Every stage of a project's lifecycle should include gathering lessons. Ask your project team to submit lessons learned during every phase of the project. This improves organizational memory of the lesson while it's still fresh in everyone's mind. On domestic projects you may be able to wait until the next phase, but on international projects the next phase may require the implementation of the lesson(s) learned and it may be too late to gather them after the fact.

KEY POINTS

■ Proficiency in project management is a mixture of science (the hard skills such as budgeting and schedule development) and art (the soft skills such as political savvy, conflict management, and interpersonal influence).

■ Project communication, especially the management of stakeholder expectations, is vitally important to the success of a project.

■ The job of the project manager is often made more difficult by the lack of formal authority. Often, project team members do not report directly to the project manager, introducing a potential conflict of interest for a team member between project work and departmental work.

■ The business world has seen scores of international company mergers, turning many projects into international endeavors. International projects require that the entire project team have an increased awareness of cultural differences among all stakeholders.

TAKE ACTION

■ *Begin building a relationship with your project sponsor* by discussing the frequency of project communication you and your sponsor will require of each other. By doing so, you'll communicate to your sponsor that you expect him or her to stay actively engaged with the project. This also provides you with an opportunity to build sponsor support through interpersonal rapport.

■ *Leverage the formal authority of the functional managers* of each of your project team members. Meet with each team member and his or her manager. In the meeting, try to agree on the amount of time the team member will devote to your project. If you can, get the functional manager's approval to provide input to the team member's performance review. And if possible, leave with a written agreement between you, the team member, and the manager.

■ *Increase how frequently international projects are measured.* Because it often takes an increased amount of time to implement corrective action on an international project, you'll need early warning signs of impending problems.

□

Endnotes

1. Project Management Institute, *A Guide to the Project Management Body of Knowledge*, 3rd ed. (Newtown Square, PA: Project Management Institute, 2004).

2. Project Management Institute, *The Standard for Portfolio Management* (Newtown Square, PA: Project Management Institute, 2006).

3. Project Management Institute, *A Guide to the Project Management Body of Knowledge*, 3rd ed. (Newtown Square, PA: Project Management Institute, 2004).

4. Terri Morrison and Wayne A. Conway, *Kiss, Bow, or Shake Hands*, 2nd ed. (Avon, MA: Adams Media, 2006).

Sean's World
Discovering a Mentor

Monday morning found Sean Kramer, an IT project manager at the financial services company Blue Skies of Denver (BSOD), traveling on Interstate 25 to his downtown Denver office. As he sat in traffic, Sean couldn't help but wonder about his future at BSOD. He had been chosen by Leah Ranson, Vice President of Corporate Strategy, to be project manager for the Sagebrush project. Leah was aware of Sean's background in IT, change management, and process reengineering, and he had made a good impression. His background seemed perfect to lead the Sagebrush project.

Sagebrush was devised by corporate headquarters to address a pressing business issue. Over the past two years, and in the last year particularly, the high-end business financial services market in which BSOD had played since its founding had leveled off. Anticipating this might indicate market saturation, Leah devised a strategy to increase sales by offering financial services like payroll processing, accounting, and client billing, coupled with customized business services like accounting workflow and vendor payment processing, that met the needs of their clients' business processes.

The BSOD strategy was to expand its operations into the small- and medium-sized business (SMB) market while simultaneously providing expanded business services to their current large corporate clients. To provide this added service, the Sagebrush project would expand the already large BSOD IT infrastructure to provide additional storage and servers for their clients to host customized financial process applications and services. This would allow their clients to reduce the overhead costs associated with those functions, and it would allow the cost of managing federally mandated regulations like Sarbanes-Oxley—a regulation ensuring accountability for a company's accounting practices—to be reduced by as much as 50 percent.

Since joining the BSOD IT department ten months ago, Sean had been able to make some valuable connections because his work as an IT project manager reached across several of the company's business units. Sean enjoyed the challenge of working among the diverse backgrounds of the varied business segments represented on the project team. But the project, even though it was only one month old, was already proving to be a major challenge for Sean and his project team. Much of his time had been spent fighting fires on a daily basis instead of directing the effort toward the much needed planning activities. The daily project firefights and seemingly endless political backstabbing and power plays made him want to run and hide. It was so bad, in fact, that he'd considered asking for another assignment within the company or even seeking employment elsewhere.

This morning, Sean was scheduled to give a project status review to his boss, Reginald "Reggie" Davis. Just the thought of it pained him. Reggie was a retired Marine master sergeant who was not interested in hearing about people-related problems associated with projects, and he was notorious for raising his voice in vicious outbursts at the slightest provocation. In his management-through-intimidation view, simply speaking in a high volume and curt tone is what it takes to inspire your team. This may have worked in the Marines, but not in a setting that relies on your ability to inspire and motivate people who do not directly report to you.

Reggie liked to call the Sagebrush project "Crazy-brush," an obvious sign that he was not a strong supporter. Perhaps Reggie thought he should have been given the project instead of Sean. Whatever the case, he was not going to be a strong supporter of Sean successfully completing the assignment unless it was going to increase his own chances for advancement as well.

For a matrix organization that aligns personnel with groups according to job skill, BSOD was unusually hierarchical, offering Reggie an environment he was very comfortable in. However, it caused others much consternation, and Sean thought it was one of the prime reasons that BSOD was unable to move quickly on opportunities. Decisions that should be made at a lower level had to be run up the chain of command, argued, and dissected before any movement was allowed. In the rapidly changing financial services industry, this was counterproductive to market mobility.

Sean decided to pull into Mariah's Magnificent Mud, a small coffee shop he'd often passed on his way to work but had never visited. It was 8:00 a.m., and Sean's presentation was scheduled for 11:00. He'd have time here to polish up his status report and presentation. Sean grabbed his laptop and entered the coffee shop the locals referred to as "The Mud." When he had settled into a booth and begun to work, a woman approached to take his order.

"May I get you something to drink and a menu?" she said.

Sean looked up from his laptop with obvious worry on his face, "Yes, I'll have a cup of coffee. No menu, thanks."

"Whoa! What's on your mind this morning, son?" she asked Sean.

"I'm presenting a project status review this morning to my boss," he replied. "And he's not such a strong supporter of this particular project or me—I can't determine which, perhaps both."

"Oh yes, the project review—I remember it well."

Sean looked at her with curiosity, "What do you mean, you remember it well?"

"Well, I've got a few years of project reviews under my belt." She shifted her weight onto the opposite leg and placed one hand on her hip as she poured Sean's coffee. "You don't think I've had this coffee shop all my life, do you?"

"This is your shop?" Sean inquired. "You're Mariah?"

"Yes, Mariah Gold. I started this shop when I retired after 30 years of project management. What's your name?"

"Sean."

"Sean, if I may ask, what is it about the review that has you so worried?"

Leaning back in the booth, Sean replied, "This is the first month of the project and I'm already two weeks behind schedule. We should've had the planning finished by now, but the team can't seem to focus long enough to get the ball rolling."

"Let me guess. They want to accomplish something besides simply planning?" replied Mariah, rolling her eyes.

"Yes, not to mention that everyone is being pulled in a million different directions by their managers."

Mariah laughed. "I see that nothing's really changed since I left the corporate world. It appears that the names and faces have changed, but the challenges remain the same. It's amazing we get anything done at all. Good luck, son."

Mariah left Sean to his thoughts and his work. As he modified the presentation, he pondered, "I have over 35 years left until I can retire. I wonder, what will I do then?" Sean awoke from his daydream and returned to the reality of his situation. He had chosen the project management profession because he appreciated the hard work it took to complete a project within budget, on schedule, and while meeting quality standards.

Sean had worked for some inept project managers during his 15-year career as a technology worker prior to becoming a project manager several years ago. He did not want to fall victim to the "halo effect"—the cognitive bias that results from one set of events and inappropriately influences perceptions of subsequent events—he'd witnessed so many times. He had seen too many engineers get promoted into positions as project managers simply because they were good engineers, even though they had little to no project management training or skills. So he spent two years pursuing a formal project management education. The time was well-spent, and he could now ascertain his project health by using earned value management, decrease the probability of catastrophe by implementing risk management, and increase the chance of success by following a well-sequenced planning and scheduling strategy.

Sean looked up just in time to see Mariah returning. "You know, I worked for more than 30 years as a project manager, and listening to your situation brings back many memories. I've learned a thing or two about project management that they don't teach you in school. Do you have a mentor?"

"Well . . . no, I don't. I guess it never occurred to me to have one."

"You seem like a nice young man. I'd like to offer my insights and experience to you in hopes that you don't make many of the same mistakes I made early in my career. Would you be interested?"

Sean thought momentarily, then responded eagerly. "Sure, why not? What would you like to do?" It was approaching 10:00 and he had to get going to the office.

"The coffee shop closes at 5:00 today; would you be interested in stopping by at 6:00?" said Mariah.

"Sure, let's make it 6:00. I'll stop back then. Thanks for the offer, Mariah."

Mariah replied, "No problem, Sean. See you then."

Sean finished the last of his coffee and headed out the door, not knowing exactly what the day would have in store for him.

Politics: Project Management Fact-of-Life

"Man is by nature a political animal."

Aristotle

We've all heard these words when talking about company politics: "If we leave politics out of this . . . ," "Leaving politics aside . . . ," and my personal favorite, "I refuse to get involved in the politics." The problem with each of these statements is that they're not grounded in reality. Politics in organizations and in project management is an unavoidable fact of life.

Political acumen is of paramount importance to the project manager because any interaction that involves a group will include some level of politics. You may choose to turn a blind eye to organizational politics, but as a project leader you do so at your own peril and at the peril of your project. This chapter focuses on the positive and negative aspects of organizational and project politics and how you can leverage politics to your advantage—and do so in an ethical way. We will also discuss key aspects of organizational culture and dynamics.

Politics: The Necessary and Vital Project Skill

When we speak of office politics, we generally do it in a negative fashion, and we're often referring to the behavior of other people, not ourselves. Politics is something *they* do, not us. In her book *Secrets to Winning at Office Politics: How to Achieve Your Goals and Increase Your Influence at Work*, Marie G. McIntyre writes, "Typically, we use the term 'playing politics' only to describe the behavior of our colleagues—never our own. *They* are sucking up, scheming, and manipulating, but *we* are building relationships, developing strategies, and opening communication channels."[1] A more fitting observation about attitudes toward organizational politics may have never been written.

The sooner we begin to understand organizational politics with a more objective eye and understand that it is neither good nor bad in itself (or that it can be good as well as bad), and that it is not something only they do and we don't, the sooner we as project managers will be able to use politics to our benefit and to the advantage of our projects. Importantly, politics can be used in a positive or negative way.

Politics is a natural fact of life when people in organizations work together. It is a way for people or groups to exert power and influence. In project management, the environment is unusually ripe for politics because, on any particular project, many stakeholders are involved. Some of them work in concert, but others come to the project with competing interests.

While the successful completion of the project should be the ultimate goal, the objectives of major stakeholders are often diametrically opposed. Identifying and managing those stakeholder interests is one of your most important jobs as a project manager. (In Chapter 4 we will take a closer look at stakeholders and their interests.)

Positive Politics

Positive use of politics can further the goals of an individual, a project, and an organization. Using political influence through sharpened interpersonal skills to the benefit of your goals and the organization is worthwhile because in most organizations, a project manager does not have the positional power or authority to remove barriers to project completion. For example, project managers must use political skill to negotiate for scarce resources—a positive use of politics. Other examples of positive politics include cultivating a network of allies to build support for a project, using influence to guide decision-makers to positive project and organizational outcomes, and leveraging an executive's positional power to help gain buy-in on projects. (Project members are more apt to come to consensus and buy in to an idea when an executive voices support for the project.)

Negative Politics

The practice of negative politics can further the goals of an individual or organization at the expense of other individuals and the organization. Some common examples of negative politics are withholding information to deceive, using threats to advance a personal goal, and using divide-and-conquer tactics (e.g., individually engaging each member of a committee to manipulate their viewpoints toward a personally favorable outcome).

So, organizational politics can be a good thing or a bad thing. How you use it will determine to a great extent whether you are successful as a project manager. Engaging in politics is part of the art of project management. If you think you're above it all, you and your projects won't succeed.

Project Management: A Political Art

Quality planning, communication management, risk management, and cost management take time to learn. The political skills a project manager needs to accomplish these and other tasks in the project lifecycle are the crux of the art of project management. Even Albert Einstein once said, "Politics is more difficult than physics."

How adept are you at politics? You can assess your own political savvy by taking the following true-or-false quiz:[2]

Politically savvy individuals . . .	T	F
1. Sometimes have to manipulate the situation to get results	☐	☐
2. Recognize that dealing with organizational politics is a necessary evil	☐	☐
3. Have superior interpersonal skills	☐	☐
4. Are more likely to work alone	☐	☐
5. Generally care a lot about ideas	☐	☐
6. Are as likely to take credit as to give it	☐	☐
7. Often take significant risks to attain important goals	☐	☐
8. Invest a great deal in making decisions more rational	☐	☐
9. Are willing to confront those they know are acting purely out of self-interest	☐	☐

This quiz is a learning tool designed to elicit your preconceived ideas about political savvy. Your answers to these questions may reveal a traditional, hierarchical, command-and-control mindset; a traditional hierarchical mindset that also recognizes the significant role of human nature in organizations; or a natural political savvy that intuitively integrates human nature and hierarchical expectations within an ethical framework. Appendix B discusses the answer for each question, and correlates the number of questions you answer correctly to where you currently fall on the political-savvy continuum.

Project management does not occur in a vacuum. To facilitate the successful delivery of our projects we must be engaged with all the actors in the project environment. You cannot effectively manage a project from behind your desk. You need all your team's interpersonal and political skills to facilitate the entire process. To this end, let's examine the project lifecycle and identify some of the political challenges we may encounter during its phases.

Politics and the Project Lifecycle

The project lifecycle is the period of time from the beginning of the project to its end, and may differ depending on the type of project. It is made up of phases that each incorporate the PMI process groups—initiating, planning, executing, controlling, and closing—a concept illustrated in Figure 2-1.[3]

The politics of a project will inevitably change during the course of the project's lifecycle. For example, resistance may be more visible during the beginning phase of the lifecycle, when people either doubt that the project can be done or ought

FIGURE 2-1 PM Process Groups and the Project Lifecycle

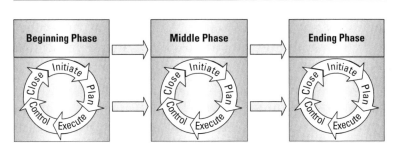

to be done, but decrease as the project progresses toward completion and appears likely to be a success.

For our purposes in this chapter, a typical project comprises three distinct phases, and for simplicity's sake, we'll call these the beginning, middle, and end phases. Each of these phases involves an array of potential political issues. Rather than an all-encompassing list of the issues and conflicts that might arise during each project phase, this is simply a view of some of the more frequently experienced political situations in which conflict tends to appear.

PMI Process Groups Versus the Project Lifecycle

To contrast the PMI process groups with the phases of the project lifecycle, consider the following example: In a typical engineering development project you may expect to move through such lifecycle phases as inception, design, development, integration, and testing. The PMI process groups (initiating, planning, executing, controlling, and closing) should be applied to each phase of the engineering project's lifecycle.

Beginning Phase

Resistance is often encountered at the beginning of a project. This is understandable when considering the ambiguity that typically surrounds project definition, with different project stakeholders having different expectations. As the project progresses, and more accurate information and definitions become available, this ambiguity will gradually decrease.

Another characteristic of the beginning phase is resource contention. In matrix organizations especially, where resource managers are required to support many projects, resource managers may be reluctant to allot resources to your project due to competing commitments. Resources are usually in finite supply and high demand, so the ability to negotiate for them is especially critical at this stage in the lifecycle. (Negotiation is covered in detail in Chapter 6.)

To aid your negotiating process and provide formal acknowledgment of the project's existence, it is critical in this beginning phase that you enlist the support of a sponsor. This is especially important for projects where the customer is your own organization rather than an external customer. Recruit this support carefully. Project sponsors must be able to relate the importance of the project back to corporate strategies and vision.

Ideally, project sponsors and stakeholders will be well aware of the importance of a project and its objectives, as well as the importance of relaying that information to others—but not always. I've personally worked in organizations

TIP: A leading cause of project failure is lack of sponsor support. Drafting a project charter that legitimizes the project and contains the signature of the project sponsor should be the first priority for the project manager prior to beginning the project.

where the project sponsor was unaware of the importance of gaining support from executives, and became upset when I solicited that support myself. This was a professional lesson learned. Educate your sponsors; do not assume that they understand the project management process.

Middle Phase

The middle phase of the lifecycle is characterized by ongoing project performance tracking, the potential for scope creep, and managing customer expectations. The major development and test activities occur during this phase. Work will be moving forward, and many course corrections will be needed. The middle phase is thus a rich environment for political play.

Quickly understanding proposed changes in scope is critical to the project during this phase. If the customer requests a change in the project's scope, pressure may be placed on the project manager to accommodate to make the customer happy. The project manager must manage customer expectations during this phase of the project to ensure that the customer is aware of the impacts their requests could have on the overall quality, cost, or schedule of the product. If expectations are not set and managed, the customer will ultimately be dissatisfied with the project outcome—even if the project is on schedule, within budget, and meets quality standards.

Since development and testing are conducted during this phase, the potential for team conflict also exists. In several projects I've witnessed, development engineers and test engineers have engaged in heated debates about the validity of tests, defects, and functions. Conflict is generally a good thing on project teams, provided it's managed to keep it healthy and constructive. Conflict that results in better quality is positive. Focus your efforts on managing the team process—not the team members.

Ending Phase

Whether the customer's expectations were managed well becomes apparent as the project team moves to gain customer acceptance. If project requirements are gathered and defined completely and successfully, expectations are met, and the product meets the needs of the customer, the ending phase should go relatively smoothly. But there are still considerations to keep in mind.

First, a key event that has the potential to bring conflict to the surface and cause political aligning is the project close-out meeting. A good practice for a project manager is to bring the core stakeholders together, "remove" everyone's rank, and take an honest look at what went right, what went wrong, and what can be carried forward to the next project and documented in a historical database. One way to remove rank is by distributing questionnaires to the team members and asking them to submit the results anonymously. Another way is to hold a meeting without managers present. Someone records notes anonymously and returns them to management.

It may be difficult to convince the project team to view the meeting as a rank-removed session. The apprehension of team members will usually surface as a reluctance to engage in honest and open dialogue. They will worry about how the people with power to give them assignments will perceive them. While being mindful of this concern, project managers should still actively mine for conflicts, issues, and concerns in order to bring them to the surface and minimize the

TIP: When leading meetings, always actively mine for conflict. Because team members are often reluctant to speak their minds, you need to be able to identify when someone is holding back an opinion or feedback. With experience and practice you'll become aware of the subtle cues that individuals are communicating. Stay observant and watch for shifting eyebrows, rolling eyes, and what people are saying through their body posture and facial expressions. When you witness such signs, ask for clarification and what the person is thinking. Keeping problems hidden will only lead to more severe confrontations later.

probability of their occurrence during the next project.

Organizational Culture

An organization is much like a living organism. The organization's pulse comprises widely accepted and shared understanding, meaning, and values. These all add up to the "personality" of an organization—or its culture. An organization's culture may be characterized by many different factors. The organization may embrace innovation and creativity, encourage teamwork, value diversity, be people-oriented, or invite risk-taking to push the technological envelope. The organizational culture is the overarching perception held by the organization's members of how business is done on a daily basis—a set of shared values. This includes how people relate to one another.

An organization may have many subcultures within the overarching culture. Subcultures may exist among different departments, hierarchical levels, or functional areas within the organization. For example, the sales and marketing team may have a culture that supports fast sales turnaround, while the engineering team may consistently want to add features to a product set.

The culture of a company may be strong or weak. A strong culture exists when core values, beliefs, and behaviors are both intensely held and widely accepted. When these characteristics are generally accepted but not intensely held, the culture is said to be weak. This is an important distinction because a strong culture has a greater influence on the behavior of its members than a weak culture. It is also more difficult to institute change in a strong culture.

Many organizational cultures will change dramatically over the next several years. Twenty-eight percent of the U.S. population consists of the Baby Boom generation—those born between 1946 and 1964.[4] This generation is set to retire over the next several years. Baby Boomer retirement will cause organizations to lose some valuable knowledge and experience. As a result, older workers may be called back to offer consultations, which may cause internal tension among those with differing core values and beliefs. For example, Baby Boomers are typically very loyal to an organization while other generations place more emphasis on finding organizations that support *their* goals.

Pros and Cons

Like many things in life (including politics, as we have noted), organizational culture has its pros and cons. A strong, shared organizational culture can enhance organizational consistency. On the negative side, certain aspects of culture can damage an organization, sometimes beyond repair.

For example, an organization may have a culture that moves very slowly due to heavily ingrained processes and procedures. That type of conservative culture may have worked at one time, but it can be a barrier to the kind of change needed to keep up with the competition. I've witnessed attempts by organizations working in industries accustomed to the slow adoption of commercial technologies to diversify their business offerings. They struggled to adapt to the changes because they didn't have an organizational culture conducive to the new venture.

Organizational culture can also pose problems for mergers and acquisitions. One merger I experienced personally—and survived to tell the story—was the 2002 merger between Hewlett Packard and Compaq. Both organizations had very strong corporate cultures that respectively served as an advantage to each. Hewlett Packard's culture was typified by analysis, planning, and finally, by decision-making—but sometimes too late. The culture of Compaq rewarded quick action—but sometimes at the expense of much needed forethought. Bringing these cultures together proved to be almost insurmountable.

A weakness in a company's culture may simply be a strength that goes too far. Cultures are ever-present in organizations and should be something for the employees to look toward for guidance. If, however, the set of values is over-stressed, negative aspects may become apparent. An organization's culture should be kept in perspective when considering strategic direction and growth.

Organizational Dynamics

Recall that one characteristic of a project is that it is unique. It isn't a plan to change the world—it is specific to a time and place and to a defined set of products and goals. (Although it may change *your* world if you're good at managing it. Your bonus may get you that beach house after all!)

Anything unique implies change that hasn't been implemented before. And change naturally challenges the status quo and creates uncertainty. The status quo is difficult to challenge in many organizations. Often, people will refer to the current state as simply "the way we do things around here." Changes to the organizational equilibrium are referred to as *organizational dynamics*.

Politics are inherently involved in organizational dynamics and change. In organizations, internal change agents typically are executives high in the organization who have a lot at stake in the change.[5] These individuals have usually risen to their level because their values are in alignment with the organization's culture. When employees who are new to the organization, and have less attachment to the status quo, initiate change—indeed, they may have been hired explicitly to shake up the status quo—political activity ensues.

Major change barriers are usually erected by those managers who have invested their entire career with a single organization. These managers may view any dynamic that challenges the status quo as a threat to their power and influence. Power struggles may determine the amount of change within an organization, as long-time career executives put up resistance. The project manager should take this into consideration when identifying a corporate project sponsor. Realize that the support for your project—because it is unique and could be charting a new path for the company—may be only lukewarm initially.

Why is change so difficult? Some typical causes of individual resistance may be insecurity, fear of the unknown ("the devil we know is better than the devil we don't know"), economic factors, and plain old habit. Some organizational causes are related to the rigidity of corporate structures (by definition, structures are built-in mechanisms to ensure stability), a perceived threat to a group's expertise, or a perceived threat to resources or power relationships within an organization.

The Project Manager as an Agent of Organizational Change

Competition among companies is fierce and intense, and the pace of technological change in today's business environment is staggering. Time-to-market of products may be the only differentiator between being a market leader or a market follower. Being beaten to market with a product launch can seriously strain an organization's ability to gain consumer confidence and product acceptance. Being first to market may ultimately allow an organization to drive the marketplace in its favor.

Project management is a sound strategy for managing change within an organization. By implementing change through a proven project management process, companies adopting such practices may realize benefits that other companies may be unable to achieve. Some key attributes of project management are enlisting the assistance of an executive-level project sponsor (change agent), driving to realistic schedules while simultaneously managing risk and quality, generating team buy-in and ownership, and managing stakeholder expectations. Each of these is geared toward aiding the organization in its far-reaching change efforts.

Project Politics and Self-Awareness

Projects are performed by people. The project manager simply cannot afford to forget this. Success will come much easier if we have the interpersonal skills to manage stakeholders effectively at all levels. It becomes much easier when we have a deep understanding of ourselves.

As we have stressed, the successful project manager is skilled in the art of politics—indirect influence, negotiation, and building networks of allies. You can enhance these abilities by possessing self-awareness. Pay attention to your abilities, emotions, and motives. Continually assess your capabilities in relation to your environment. What is the political lay of the land? Do I have an appropriate negotiating position to gain the support my project demands? Are my skills sufficient given the environment I'm operating in? What do I do well that will further the goals and objectives of my project?

To help you understand your political self-awareness, consider each statement below. The more statements that you consider true, the more you'll need to work on increasing your political self-awareness.

	T	F
1. I find it difficult to work with people I do not like.	☐	☐
2. I frequently and easily find myself in arguments with colleagues.	☐	☐
3. I do not understand the motives of others, or I am at least suspicious of them.	☐	☐
4. I believe that the real power usually lies at the top of the hierarchy.	☐	☐
5. I do not influence others as easily as I'd like.	☐	☐
6. I feel I am treated unfairly.	☐	☐
7. I feel I am often taken advantage of.	☐	☐
8. My true value is not recognized by those in power.	☐	☐
9. When I feel I'm being attacked, I am unsure about how best to respond.	☐	☐

Project managers should take time at the beginning of a project's lifecycle to perform an introspective inventory. This does not have to be anything more than taking a few moments to sit alone quietly and ponder our questions and listen to our subconscious. I'm not suggesting that we all become Zen masters and learn the art of meditation. But I am suggesting that we think about our past experiences, what we've learned from them, and how we can apply these lessons to the project we're about to undertake. We must maintain confidence in ourselves but also take care to not deceive ourselves about our weak points, abilities, or needs as individuals.

It's also a good practice to take the time to reflect like this during the project. This will be especially true when you encounter tough problems and issues. Take some time away from your project environment to think, reassess, and plan. Often, answers to your questions will come during this introspective time. Occasionally, you may realize that you are amplifying issues out of proportion. Reflection and introspection offer us an opportunity to find the strength within ourselves to face the inevitable challenges that lie ahead.

KEY POINTS

- Projects and organizations are rife with politics. To ignore the political element of project work is to accept less than total control of your project's—and your own—destiny.

- As a project progresses through its lifecycle, the dynamics of the political environment will ebb and flow. Because of this, a project manager must continually assess the political environment.

- The political environment will be affected by the dynamics of the organization and the business climate. The company's history, culture, and acceptance of change will also have an impact on the project's political situation.

■ To work effectively in the project's and organization's political environments, you must have a high level of self-awareness. The effective project politician must be aware of his or her strengths, weaknesses, and abilities.

TAKE ACTION

■ *Become visible.* Do not spend the bulk of your day behind your desk. Make your contributions and efforts across the stakeholder community visible. Invisible efforts and contributions carry no political value.

■ *Make a list of those you view as your project's allies* and the reasons why. What else can you do to build a strong network of allies? Ask each core member of your project team to do the same. Analyze the results in a team forum. The outcome of this exercise can be quite eye-opening.

■ *Take a personality assessment.* There are several good ones on the market today. The assessment I've found to be very credible and backed by extensive research is the Winslow report.[6] This assessment measures 24 personality traits and identifies the areas you need to pay attention to.

☐

Endnotes

1. Marie G. McIntyre, Ph.D., *Secrets to Winning at Office Politics* (New York: St. Martin's Press, 2005).
2. This section is adapted from *Political Savvy,* by Joel R. DeLuca, Ph.D., http://www.politicalsavvy.com/docs/quiz.html (accessed March 29,

2007). Reprinted with permission from Evergreen Business Group (Copyright © 2007).

3. Project Management Institute, *A Guide to the Project Management Body of Knowledge*, 3rd ed. (Newtown Square, PA: Project Management Institute, 2004).

4. Sophie M. Korczyk, Ph.D., "Baby-Boomers Head for Retirement," *Journal of Financial Planning*, http://www.fpanet.org/journal/articles/2001_Issues/jfp0301-art12.cfm (accessed April 6, 2006).

5. Stephen P. Robbins, *Organizational Behavior*, 10th ed. (Upper Saddle River, NJ: Prentice Hall, 2003).

6. Winslow Research Institute, *Winslow Reports*, http://www.winslow reports.com (accessed March 2, 2007).

Sean's World
The Drama

Sean arrived at The Mud at six o'clock, as instructed.

"Grab a seat and make yourself at home, Sean. I'll be right there. How did your project review go?" Mariah asked as she made her way to the front of the shop.

Sean slid into the same booth he had sat in that morning. "Well, the review actually went better than I expected. It was something that occurred this afternoon that took me by surprise. Right after lunch, one of my team members told me about some of the things being said about Sagebrush in one of our business segments."

"What do you mean?" Mariah inquired.

"Lynn Williams, my marketing team lead, told me about some rumors she'd heard. Because our project reaches across departmental boundaries, which usually doesn't happen at BSOD, several departments are positioning to be viewed as the one leading Sagebrush."

Mariah looked at Sean with curiosity, "Does this surprise you?"

"Actually, yes it does! I'd like to believe that we're all one company here. I've been appointed the project manager. Why must we have all these politics?"

The hallway talk at BSOD was that the financial services department was not in alignment with the project. Sean suspected that Shane Thomas, a financial services representative, was the person responsible for poisoning the well. Shane was inwardly skeptical about the Sagebrush project and didn't fully accept the strategy behind it. He saw the advantage of expanding services to the large clients, but believed that expanding into the SMB market would further tax the company's already burdened resources. The fact that BSOD was planning to add business process reengineering and a suite of customizable software to its service offerings, two areas in which the company had limited expertise, only served to add to his concern.

"Sean, can I ask you a question?"

"Sure," Sean said with a slight hesitation.

"What did you do before you were a project manager?"

"I worked as a systems administrator."

"Did you experience politics in that job?"

"Sure, but not to the degree that I have since becoming a project manager," Sean replied.

"I see."

Sean looked confused. "Why?"

"Actually, Sean, the higher you go in an organization, the more politics you'll encounter and have to deal with."

Sean shifted uneasily in his seat. "I just want to do what's right and not worry about the politics."

"Please," Mariah replied while rolling her eyes. "Sean, that's the most naïve statement I think I've ever heard."

At this point Sean was second-guessing his willingness to be mentored by Mariah. He did not enjoy controversy and was not a confrontational person. His voice was filled with contempt. "What are you talking about, Mariah? What makes you say that?"

"Let me tell you a story, Sean. Early in my career I was employed by an accounting software company. I was tasked with managing the development of a new product line. Actually, it was my first experience in a project leadership role. I was promoted to project manager because I was always able to bring my tasks to completion on time. Back then I had the same view of project and organizational politics as you do now. I only wanted to do what's right without getting involved in all of the politics related to the project. I thought that keeping the project on track and moving would be enough to ensure its success. I couldn't have been more misguided. Look, project management is a unique profession. It provides an environment ripe for politics. Projects usually involve lots of stakeholders, and some of them have a lot to lose if the project succeeds. This was the case in my situation. It seemed everything was going fine until a major checkpoint review rolled around."

Mariah took a deep breath and continued. "Right before the review, my boss told me the project had been cancelled. He said the development costs had been too much for the organization to bear, and upper management had decided to scrap my project and go with another product. I later found out the real reason. My project was a threat to one of the company's lower-end software products. If we had been successful, the group developing the lower-end product would've been disbanded and forced to find other jobs within the company or be laid off. I discovered they'd put a case together showing the development costs of my project over time and how they compared with the costs of upgrading their product to be in line with current technology. When I found out my project was cancelled, I was crushed. How could management ignore the obvious technical advantage my product had? Why did they choose to end its development without hearing my side of the story?"

Sean perceived the impact the event had obviously had on Mariah. "I'm sorry Mariah, but how does that relate to what Lynn Williams told me today?"

"From that point on, I decided to never again ignore the environment my projects existed in. I'm going to help you do the same, Sean. If you ignore the interdepartmental power struggle going on right now, you could be well on your way to a doomed project."

Sean replied pleadingly, "So, what do you propose that I do?"

Mariah responded, "At this point, I don't know. What environment is your project being conducted in?"

"What environment?"

"Yes, what environment? What is it like at BSOD? What's the culture? How are relationships within the project team? Have these people worked together before? How large is your core team? What are their personalities like? What's the overall sentiment regarding the project? Who is your sponsor? How vocal are they?"

Sean was amazed and tried to ponder the torrent of questions. Only being at BSOD for ten months, Sean realized he should've spent more time studying the organizational culture, the dynamics, and the organizational politics. Mariah had so many questions, and he had so few answers. How could he possibly get a grasp of the situation in time to implement Sagebrush?

"Mariah, I can definitely see I've got some work to do here. I can't answer all those questions right now. I think you've given me some homework."

"OK Sean, take some time and answer the questions. Talk to your team members. Observe your surroundings and how people interact. Write your answers down in a journal to refer back to them if you need to."

Sean and Mariah both had a long day ahead of them. It was getting late as Sean finished his coffee and asked, "When would you like to meet again, Mariah?"

"It sounds like you've got your work cut out for you on this Sagebrush project. Why don't you stop by when you need advice, Sean? And in the meantime, find a spot and some time to do some thinking and reflecting. I've found that it often helps to sit quietly and listen to myself. Answers will often appear to me, and I always find self-assurance. Perhaps you will find this to be the case for you also."

"Thanks very much, Mariah. I'll do that."

Sean left the coffee shop eager to begin his new assignment. He was already looking forward to his next meeting at The Mud.

Conflict: Don't Fear the Inevitable

"Restlessness and discontent are the first necessities of progress."

Thomas A. Edison

Early in my career I had little, if any, awareness of the utility of conflict. As far as I was concerned, conflict was something to be avoided at all costs. When I became a project manager, I began to appreciate the conflict process, and I've grown aware of the need to proactively manage it rather than avoid it. Perhaps as a result of personal maturation or an increased understanding of the organizational process—probably both—my awareness of impending conflict has enhanced my ability to successfully lead projects. I no longer wait for conflict to find me. In fact, I now recognize it as a natural stage of the development, project, and team process. I no longer react to conflict with fear as I once did.

The Necessity of Project Conflict

Conflict is a difficult topic to address because the tendency in human nature is to avoid it. After all, who wants to be in an unpleasant interaction?

But conflict is inevitable, especially because project team members often come from different functional areas. There are also executive-level sponsors, customers, and various other stakeholders, each with differing interests and goals. Inevitably, those interests will come into conflict at some point in the project lifecycle. Additionally, managing an intersection of the triple constraints—cost, time, and quality—is another critical source of conflict among project stakeholders. For example, an engineer on a project team may want a specific technical solution to a problem, but that solution may come at a cost unacceptable to the customer or project sponsor.

Research has shown that as a manager you can expect to spend more than 40 percent of your time negotiating and reaching agreement between stakeholders when conflicts occur.[1] This is a large drain on your time and energy. For this reason, you must proactively manage conflict and actively mine for areas of conflict early in the project lifecycle. Don't let things fester and pop up later.

We can deal with conflict in one of two ways. We can choose to handle it poorly (or ignore it altogether), or we can recognize it and address it directly in an open and proactive manner. But, again, here's the key: Understanding and accepting that conflict is inevitable in project management is the first step in addressing it.

When approached properly, conflict has the potential to become a positive driving force on a project team, motivating and bonding team members, inspiring creativity, and increasing morale, all of which reduce employee turnover. If dealt with poorly (or ignored), however, conflict can tear a project team apart, increase employee turnover, drain energy, and decrease the chance of project success. In extreme cases, it may even lead to physical violence.

> **TIP:** Emotional conflict stemming from issues such as personality clashes, ego, and anger can be very destructive and difficult to resolve. Emotional conflict has the potential to tear a team apart. If your team is confronted with emotional conflict, intervene quickly to get to the heart of the matter. In extreme cases, it may be necessary to bring in an external mediator to help the team work through the issue(s).

Because conflict can have such disparate impacts, and sometimes only a fine line separates the two, project managers should add conflict management, facilitation, and interpersonal skills to their toolboxes and always strive to increase their proficiency in those skills.

The likelihood of conflict and the forms it can take will vary depending on the type or complexity of your project. It may also vary with the project phase you're currently operating in. Let's examine some of the sources and types of conflicts that are most likely to arise in each project phase. To do so, we can look at each of the project process groups as defined in the *PMBOK® Guide.*[2]

Source of Conflict in Project Process Groups

The *PMBOK® Guide* describes five process groups—initiating, planning, executing, controlling, and closing—that should all be iterated (repeated) through each phase of the project lifecycle. For each project process group there are differing expectations from varying stakeholder groups, and it's important to understand how these expectations will change as the lifecycle progresses from phase to phase.

Initiating Process

During initiation, it's critical to bring conflict into the open. This is the time to establish a project culture that promotes open, frank communication and invites constructive and healthy conflict. Keep in mind that the environment for success is ultimately set in the beginning phase of the project, not at the end. Impress upon your team that conflict is not to be avoided. If you don't, it will fester until it comes to a head at a critical project date. Further, it's important to establish communication during initiation because this is when there can be the most ambiguity and the most intense competition for resources. Also, at this stage you are bringing together for the first time a team whose members you may not know and who do not know each other.

Reducing Ambiguity. The initiating process is a time when ambiguity can be high. Typically, a few critical stakeholders, such as the customer or the project sponsor, will believe they are absolutely clear about the project and what its ultimate product should be. The success of the project will depend to a large degree on how well they communicate this understanding to you and the project team. But all too often the customer or sponsor does *not* have a clear expectation for a project. As the project manager, if you question the sponsor or customer, you will often elicit contradictory requirements, unclear details, and areas of inconsistency. In short, the customer or sponsor may know what they want but not be able to communicate it. Or, even though they may think they have clarity, they may simply not know what they really want. This ambiguity can easily lead to conflict later on, when the sponsor comes to you and says, "But that's not what we really wanted."

Competing for Scarce Resources. The initiation process is also characterized by a struggle for key—and limited—resources such as personnel and budget, identification and clarification of project administrative procedures, and the determination of the project objective and success criteria. Essentially, this phase involves all activities necessary to set the stage for the planning phase of the project.

Knowing Your Team. You will be leading a project team composed of individuals you may or may not know well. Here's a practical tip for every project manager, or any leader for that matter: Take some time to get to know your project team members. I mean *really* know and understand them as individuals. Let's not forget that projects are performed by people; your ultimate job as a project manager is to connect with these people, and to lead them and your project to success. Their success is your success. Work to find out about them, genuinely. Where are they from? What are their likes and dislikes? Do they have children? How many? How old? What's their educational background? What's their professional background? What hobbies do they enjoy? How do they spend their time off?

Taking time to get to know your team members will give you valuable insight into them as people. You can gain critical insights on how to connect with and engage them. Personally, I do not think you can be a consistently effective project leader without having a caring sense for people. And there is a significant side benefit: You'll be a better person because of it.

Planning Process

While ambiguity typifies the initiating process, negotiation and communication characterize the planning process. Getting the resource manager's support to commit resources to plan the project is of critical importance during this period. The project manager should work to foster open communication and a good working relationship with the resource managers to enhance the chance of success.

Project managers often underestimate the pressure that resource managers are under. Typically, resource managers have department-level goals they're accountable for, as well as several projects competing for their finite supply of human capital. In addition, the resource manager must work to foster an environment that enables personal and professional growth for their direct reports. Not surprisingly, the resource manager has a high likelihood of facing off with several project sponsors competing for scarce resources. Keeping this in mind will go a long way toward helping you empathize with the resource manager's situation and enhance the ability to foster a positive working relationship. Showing empathy and genuine situational awareness of another's point of view goes a long way toward garnering support and buy-in. However, you must be genuine. Attempts to show disingenuous caring will be transparent. (In Chapter 5 we'll discuss nonverbal communication and will illustrate why false empathy is so transparent, particularly on the subconscious level.)

Executing and Controlling Processes

Execution and control processes are iterative and integrated. During this time, project managers should keep communication at the forefront to be fully engaged in the project. Typical situations occurring during this period that have great potential for conflict are the realization of unforeseen risks, delays due to technical problems, and the handoff of key deliverables between project team members. Conflict can arise if stakeholder expectations are not managed appropriately.

The potential for conflict also increases as individual team members are under immense pressure to perform. Fast-approaching deadlines, decreasing budgets, and increased stakeholder pressure can take a large toll on the project team, which may result in shorter tempers.

Closing Process

First-time project managers typically fall into the trap of believing the closing process holds the least amount of potential for project conflict. I know I certainly held the same misconception. However, as the project nears completion and product delivery dates loom, pressure to perform increases on the team. Team members are completing individual tasks, and the pressure to meet scheduled dates and milestones is incredibly high. And by this point you may have a team that is feeling tired and overworked.

Depending on the organizational structure surrounding the project, different types of anxiety manifest themselves as a project reaches the defining closeout phase. In a functional organization, this element of anxiety is less than in other organizational structures because each team member is typically involved in multiple projects simultaneously, preventing worry about reassignment as projects complete.

Matrix project environments have a similar dynamic, because team members feel confident their functional managers will assign them to one project after another. As a result, they feel mixed loyalties as the mundane and unchallenging administrative tasks they're performing to close one project seem less stimulating than the challenges awaiting them on the next project.

Projectized organizations may use several sub-organizations to complete projects, and in many cases employees and contractors may be let go upon project completion. As a result, project teams may experience a high level of anxiety because members may feel they've essentially worked themselves out of a job by completing project tasks.

TIP: Ensure that each phase of the project is closed properly before initiating the next phase. As part of the closing process, gather lessons-learned to help ensure the next project phase is executed more efficiently.

Types of Conflict

Conflict has the potential to build morale, increase team cohesiveness, and enhance creativity. Or it can be a force capable of destroying collaboration, increasing employee turnover, and damaging personal and professional relationships. Let's look at both possibilities.

Constructive Conflict

In Chapter 1 we noted that most of us think of conflict as a destructive element. But we have to stretch our thinking a bit and realize that not all conflict is bad. In fact, some conflict can be good.

Conflict is constructive and healthy when it results in increased innovation and creativity, arouses increased interest and curiosity on the part of team members, improves the quality of decisions, and provides an environment that encourages the airing of problems. By working through healthy conflict, you can cultivate an environment of decreased tension.[3] As project managers, we need to be attentive to our environments and look for situations that offer opportunities to encourage constructive conflict.

Consider the following example: While seated in a project team meeting, one member of the team offers a suggestion to help solve an ongoing issue with one of the deliverables. As the team member speaks, you notice another member slump down in his chair and roll his eyes. You now have an opportunity to encourage constructive conflict. Many times, the person demonstrating subtle signs of disagreement will not voice any concerns. The best approach I've found to deal with this situation is to have the person express his or her thoughts after the other team member has finished speaking. Do not ask them—*tell* them you want to know what they're thinking. This will not only show you are an active listener, but it will also demonstrate that you care about everyone's thoughts, whether positive or negative.

Be aware and focus at all times, particularly in meetings. A very intelligent and intuitive mentor I once had advised me, "Be here now." By "being here," you are alert to the moment. Foster an environment that encourages communication and the open sharing of ideas in a nonjudgmental way. However, keep in mind that to do this you must also accept when someone challenges you, and avoid passing judgment on that individual. We are the authors of our environments, so choose to let your environment become a positive and healthy one.

Destructive Conflict

Destructive conflict has the potential to be devastating to the project environment and, ultimately, the health of the project, the organization, and its employees. For our purposes, destructive conflict can be defined as any conflict scenario that produces no positive outcome for the persons in conflict, the project, or the organization.

Destructive conflict may also lead to unethical political play. For example, consider the situation in which the team member rolled his eyes at his colleague's suggestion. Had the team member not been confronted by the observant project manager, he might have left at the end of the meeting determined to undermine any outcome or decision made during the meeting. Undermining the work of others is unethical political play. Ultimately, others may find out, which can lead to additional conflict and damage the personal relationship.

Conflict will happen, regardless of the amount of effort we put forth to stifle it. If it is not identified and brought into the open, potentially healthy and constructive conflict can morph into destructive conflict. Become vigilant of your team members' personalities and aware of the personal interactions on your project.

Conflict Resolution Modes

When faced with conflict, it is helpful to be aware of our personal behaviors and how we approach conflict management. While each of us has a preferred style of confronting and facilitating conflict, the preferred approach should be tailored to the type of conflict. The Thomas-Kilmann Conflict Mode Instrument (TKI)[4] describes five basic modes for resolving conflict—competing, avoiding, accommodating, collaborating, and compromising (see Figure 3-1).

Competing

The competing mode is essentially a win-at-any-cost approach. It is characterized by a high level of assertiveness and a low level of cooperation. In this mode you essentially impose your authority, stand your ground, and assert your opinion(s). This conflict mode is most appropriate when very quick and particularly difficult decisions need to be made. It is also useful when protecting your interests.

FIGURE 3-1 Five Modes for Resolving Conflict

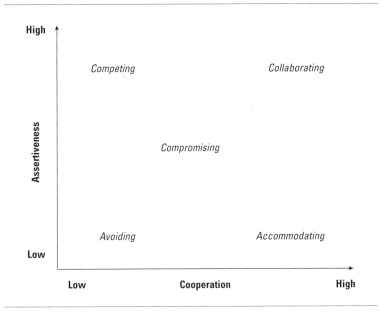

TIP: A tendency exists in teams to discuss issues and conflicts in a sequential manner. However, several studies have shown that issues discussed sequentially only serve to reduce the chance that the team will identify potentially beneficial trade-offs between issues.[5] When discussing important issues, stick to the matter at hand and avoid dredging up old history.

Avoiding

The avoiding mode is fairly self-explanatory and is characterized by withdrawing and removing oneself from conflict situations, changing the subject when tough or unpopular decisions are faced, and moving toward overall ignorance of conflict. Very low assertiveness coupled with low cooperation is the identifying characteristic. You may wonder if this mode is ever appropriate. Actually, the avoiding mode is an effective technique to employ when issues arise that are of low importance to the overall goals of the project, or when you need to buy time when you're in a position of low power or influence.

Accommodating

Low assertiveness and high cooperation characterize the accommodating mode. For someone in a position of little influence or authority, accommodating is like being a good soldier who follows orders and obeys persons in the higher levels of power no matter what they command. When using the accommodating mode, you are essentially yielding your needs or desires to the other party in the conflict. This mode may be used during times when you need to create a sense of good will or keep the peace to advance the project, or when the outcome of the conflict is not critical to you or the project.

Collaborating

The collaborating mode is the equilibrium point in conflict resolution modes. It is characterized by a high level of assertiveness and a high level of cooperation. When true collaboration is occurring, both parties are in a creative state working together to solve an issue in a way that will best suit each. If time permits, this may be the preferred method of conflict resolution. However, a very thorough understanding of the other party and a great deal of time and energy are required to collaborate well.

Very important issues that impact the entire project lifecycle warrant the time and energy of collaboration to reach agreement. For example, working through how best to communicate issues and manage risks throughout the project both warrant collaboration, because they will impact the entire team through the project lifecycle. The skills required for collaboration are active listening and attention to detail, and there must be a non-threatening environment in which both parties feel it is safe to participate.

Compromising

Compromising means working with moderate levels of assertiveness and cooperation. Compromising is used quite frequently in negotiation. When two parties compromise, both are essentially making concessions to come to a consensus that is acceptable to both in order to resolve the conflict. If you're dealing with issues that are moderately important to you, the project, or your team, you may want to work to compromise with the party in conflict. Compromise is also used when temporary solutions are required to meet time constraints.[6]

Generational Differences

One source of potential conflict is a generational gap between project and organizational team members. We are all familiar with the generation gaps described in psychology and family counseling literature, and when we are adolescents, we hear (sometimes from our parents) of the gap between us and the generation before us. In the workplace, however, generation gaps are commonly overlooked, especially in the project environment. Yet generation gaps can exist in the workplace, particularly today. Never before have workers from four distinct generations been employed side by side as they are at this time. As young professionals from Generation Y (millennials) begin to move into the workforce, they're entering a workplace also populated by Generation X, Baby Boomers, and traditionalists. Each of these generations has its own way of doing things.

To understand the potential sources of conflict among these generations, we need to understand some of the perceptions held by older and younger workers. Notice that I said *perceptions.* I'm not concerned whether these perceptions are true. We need simply to understand that these are perceptions that are held, right or wrong, and can be the root of conflict. These age-based perceptions are proliferating because younger workers are working alongside colleagues belonging to their parents' generation.[7] Because the world has changed drastically over the past 60 years, the generations can have drastically different viewpoints about life and work.

Each generation's view of the world has been shaped by the environment it grew up in. The differences in environments have been pronounced due to the rapid technological and social changes that have taken place over the past 60 years or so, and have led to radically different ways of thinking. For example, where a worker from Generation X might not think twice about throwing out an old piece of equipment, a traditionalist, who has grown up in the post-World War II era, may see this act as wasteful because they are more accustomed to saving things.

Typical, hasty generalizations made by older workers about their younger colleagues are that they're lazy, not loyal to the company, and typically don't take advice easily.[8] Alternatively, younger workers hold the perception that their older colleagues won't accept change, are not generally tech-savvy, and follow the corporate hierarchy in an unquestioning manner. These perceptions can sometimes throw a wrench into the cogs of your project.

To help overcome some of these perceptions, work to actively engage your project teams in collaborative events. If junior team members are working alongside senior members on your project team, identify possible mentoring relationships that can promote team cohesiveness. Often, mentors themselves have just as much to learn in these type of collaborative relationships. Mentoring can aid your project by bringing junior members up the learning curve more quickly and helping mentors see the positive in the junior members.

KEY POINTS

- Most of us are not fond of conflict. However, each one of us must realize that conflict is inevitable in project work. Do not fear conflict. Instead, mine for it. Combining diverse individuals, each with different thoughts and approaches, is what thrusts solutions into view. Working to see things from a different angle is crucial to innovation, and conflict is the catalyst of innovation.

- Ignoring conflict will only delay the situation and amplify its impact. Left unattended, differences of opinion can fester to the point where they emerge as emotional conflict and can tear a project team apart at the seams.

■ Project conflict will change depending on the phase in the project lifecycle and the project process group being executed. Understand what the most likely cause of conflict is, depending on where you're at in the project.

TAKE ACTION

■ *If you are the conflict facilitator, be aware of others' body language.* The face, posture, and tone will often tell you what a person is thinking.

■ *When conflict occurs, discuss it openly with the group.* Do not allow conflict to lie unattended for too long. Address issues when they're fresh in everyone's mind.

■ *Be cautious of reaching resolutions too easily or quickly.* Each person or group in conflict will need time to consider the proposed compromises and the impact of each. Answers that come too quickly often mask the true issue(s).

■ *Do not be afraid to laugh.* I'm a firm believer that laughter is the best medicine. Being able to laugh can relieve tension between parties and bring to light solutions that may not have been previously considered.

☐

Endnotes

1. John Ford, "Workplace Conflict: Facts and Figures," *International Academy of Mediators,* http://www.mediate.com/articles/Ford1.cfm (accessed April 10, 2006).

2. Project Management Institute, *A Guide to the Project Management Body of Knowledge*, 3rd ed. (Newtown Square, PA: Project Management Institute, 2004).

3. Stephen P. Robbins, *Organizational Behavior*, 10th ed. (Upper Saddle River, NJ: Prentice Hall, 2003).

4. Kenneth W. Thomas and Ralph H. Kilmann, *Thomas-Kilmann Conflict Mode Instrument* (Mountainview, CA: CPP Inc., 2001).

5. Although several studies reinforce this statement, one of the most intriguing arguments is presented in a paper by L. R. Weingart, R. Bennett, and J. F. Brett titled, "The Impact of Consideration of Issues and Motivational Orientation on Group Negotiation Process and Outcome," *Journal of Applied Psychology*, 78:504–517, 1993.

6. The Foundation Coalition, *Understanding Conflict and Conflict Management*, http://www.foundationcoalition.org/publications/brochures/conflict.pdf (accessed April 10, 2006).

7. S. R. Rhodes, "Age-Related Differences in Work Attitudes and Behavior," *Psychological Bulletin*, 93:328–367, 1983.

8. Ibid.

Sean's World
What's My Priority?

Sean got to the conference room at 9:05 a.m., five minutes late but still the first to arrive. As Sean finished setting up the computer and projector over the next several minutes, his project team came in one by one. Finally, the meeting began at 9:15. Twenty-five percent of the meeting time had already elapsed before the meeting even began.

Sean opened, "How is everyone doing today?"

"Fine," the group replied without much enthusiasm.

Sean hesitated while gathering his thoughts, "Let's start by going around the table and have each of us lay out where we are in each portion of the project schedule. Lynn, why don't you start?"

"No updates from marketing this week. All is going fine."

"OK, Lynn, thanks," said Sean. "How about financial services, Shane?"

"I haven't had a chance to work on Sagebrush this week, Sean. I've been helping my boss with one of our major accounts."

Sean looked dismayed and responded quickly, "What do you mean? Can you explain?"

"Sure. Our ADO account needed some servicing and my boss wanted me to help."

"Then WHY didn't you INFORM me?" Sean replied sharply. "You've got a requirements deliverable that IT and marketing are waiting on from you so they can begin work. If you're not engaged, the entire schedule is slipping. Your boss committed you to this project, and I expect you to be available to work on your tasks. You're are on the critical path, Shane."

Shane shifted in his chair and crossed his arms. "I have a few things on my plate, most of which are higher priority than this project."

The rest of the core team had similar reports for Sean, which only served to irritate him more. Out of frustration, he ended the meeting 20 minutes early. The rest of the day was spent fuming in his office and reviewing the aggressive project schedule to find out what the delays meant in relation to the end date of the project. Would he be able to come up with some ingenious recovery plan?

Sean went to meet Mariah at The Mud after work. Mariah greeted him as he walked into the coffee shop.

"Welcome, Sean. Good to see you again."

"Thanks Mariah. Good to see you as well," Sean said as he slumped in the booth.

"You look like you're carrying the weight of the world on your shoulders, Sean. Is everything OK?"

"If by OK you mean is my schedule slipping and is my team member on the critical path too busy working other priorities to work my project? Then, yes, I'm OK."

"What happened today?"

"It was my weekly team meeting. I had very poor input from my core team and was told by my financial services lead, Shane Thomas, that he spent the entire week working on another project for his boss which was higher priority. Well, I got pretty angry and raised my voice a few decibels. I explained how strategic this project is to the company and how important it is to complete on time. I ended the meeting early, without resolution to the problem," Sean said as he looked at the concerned expression on Mariah's face.

Mariah weighed in on what she'd just heard, "Sean, do you have an executive sponsor?"

"Yes, I do. Leah Ranson. I've told you about her. She's the vice president for corporate strategy."

"How important is the Sagebrush project to your organization?" she asked.

"It's very important. BSOD is going to be investing several million dollars in it over the next year. It's also the execution vehicle for the company's entire growth strategy. Leah told me that herself."

"Has Leah expressed this to your team?"

"No, she hasn't," he replied.

"I see," Mariah said as she pondered momentarily. "It appears to me there's no clear vision for the rest of your team about what the Sagebrush project means to the company and how important it is for future growth. Because of this, you're experiencing a conflict of competing priorities. It's obviously been made very clear in your mind how important the Sagebrush project is, but your team does not have this same clarity. Do you have a project charter?"

"Yes, we do. It was signed by Leah as the sponsor," said Sean.

"That's a good beginning. But it's not enough."

Sean furrowed his brow in a confused manner and replied, "It's not?"

"No. You need sponsor visibility. You need to get Leah in front of your team as soon as you can, preferably while today's meeting is still fresh in everyone's mind. I suggest you also get her to draft an email to the manager of everyone on your core team. It will help give them a perspective on the importance of the project and help you get the resources you need. Sean, anything less than that will not do. You must get Leah engaged. It will make your job much easier if she is."

"I'll do that, Mariah. She gets into the office early like me. I'll try to get her when she comes in and discuss the situation with her. Hopefully, I can get some time on her calendar for her to speak to my project team. Her calendar fills up quickly."

"That's a good idea, Sean. If the project is really important to her as a sponsor, she'll make the time."

Mariah sat up in the booth, propping her elbows on the table, "Now, let's discuss this little tirade you went on during your meeting today."

"It was definitely uncharacteristic behavior for me," replied Sean.

"Sean, these people need to be able to approach you. How can you possibly expect them to bring you bad news when they believe you'll react negatively?"

"That makes a lot of sense, Mariah. But what can I do about my natural reactions?"

Mariah hesitated momentarily to ponder his question and replied, "You must be a fighter."

"A fighter? What do you mean?"

"I faced several situations during my career like the one you experienced today. It's very frustrating to be under the extreme pressure of tightening deadlines, shrinking budgets, and competing priorities. You interpreted what occurred in the meeting today as a threat to you."

Sean looked confused. "What do you mean? I don't understand. I didn't feel threatened."

"Yes, I understand you didn't feel physically threatened. But your brain doesn't know the difference. It only senses

the pressure you're under and interprets it as a threat—
which explains your reaction."

"What can I do to change that?"

"That's the good news," said Mariah. "You will be able to
intercept the reaction if you can make yourself aware of it.
The trick to doing this is two-fold. First, don't react instinctively. You must become aware of your reaction tendency
and block it by thinking through the situation. It's easier
said than done, which brings me to the second part. You
must practice this until your natural response is to think
before you act."

Sean was beginning to get a sense of what she was telling
him. He thought momentarily about the morning's meeting
and asked, "Mariah, could you give me an example of how
I should've responded this morning? What would you have
done?"

"What I would have done with Shane is this: I would have
thanked him for his honest reply and asked him for his plan
for this week's activities. Afterward, I would've spoken to
his manager about the project's priority. I also would have
worked to ensure Leah would be actively engaged with
the team."

"You make it sound so simple, Mariah. It's never quite that
easy in practice."

"Actually, Sean, it usually is. Solutions to our problems are
usually right at our fingertips if only we'd take the time and
expend the effort to see them. Now, I've got to finish get-

ting this place cleaned up. Swing by tomorrow evening. I want to share my thoughts with you on another aspect of projects that has a profound impact on success—that is, if we take the time and expend the effort required to get a firm understanding of our surroundings and environment before moving forward."

Sean took his last sip of coffee and opened the door. "Good night, Mariah. Thank you."

"You're welcome, Sean. Hang in there."

Project Stakeholders

The Project Management Institute (PMI) defines a project stakeholder as "a person or organization (e.g., customer, sponsor, performing organization, or the public) that is actively involved in the project, or whose interests may be positively or negatively affected by execution or completion of the project. A stakeholder may also exert influence over the project and its deliverables."[1]

The role of stakeholder may be filled by individuals, groups, or organizations. A stakeholder may also fill more than one role. In the case of an internal project, for example, the performing organization may also be the customer. Such is the case in most IT projects.

The PMI definition calls attention to the fact that stakeholders exert influence over the project and its deliverables. For this reason, as a project manager you must constantly work to identify the project stakeholders and understand the influence that each stakeholder brings to the project. Then you must manage the expectations of those stakeholders. This is not a one-time activity or something to perform only at the initiation of a project. Stakeholder identification and management is an iterative process that should be taken seriously, for the results can sway the outcome of a project.

As project managers, we have the daunting task of communicating with stakeholders regularly, to manage their expectations and facilitate the resolution of conflicts between them. Engaging two stakeholders with opposing viewpoints and motives, while attempting to meet the expectations of each, is not uncommon. As we stressed in Chapter 1, project managers must understand the environment in which their projects exist. Stakeholders are the key actors in that environment.

The Stakeholder Management Process

It's entirely possible to deliver a project on schedule, stay within budget, meet or exceed quality standards, and yet find that the project is still be viewed as a failure by one or more stakeholders. Stakeholder management, especially managing expectations, will help lessen the chance of this occurring.

While the ultimate responsibility for dealing with stakeholders rests on your shoulders as the project manager, the process is really a team activity. Project team members can provide valuable insight and may have a great deal more information about individual stakeholders than you do. As noted, stakeholder management is a repetitive process throughout the project lifecycle, so engage the team members at each stage. As the project progresses, new stakeholders may materialize while others may change their expectations or behaviors. As stakeholders change, so must your management of them. Because of this, performing an analysis of stakeholder interests and assembling a management and response plan only at the beginning of a project is insufficient. Figure 4-1 illustrates a process for stakeholder management.

Identifying Stakeholders

The process of identifying project stakeholders—carried out iteratively and with the collaboration of team members—must

FIGURE 4-1 Stakeholder Management Process

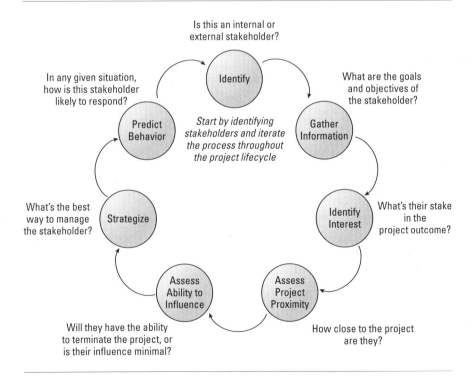

reach beyond the organization performing the project and should be as comprehensive as possible. Most projects will consist of external persons or groups with a vested interest in the outcome of your project. For example, some external stakeholder groups that are typically overlooked during this process are competitors, political groups, and external suppliers. Competitors have a stake in your project's outcome because it may impact their position in the market and the success of their own organizations. Figure 4-2 provides a sample list of project stakeholders.

The list of typical stakeholders in Figure 4-2 is not an exhaustive one. When you brainstorm with your team and prepare your own list, think widely and include anyone or any organization that will be impacted by your project or have an influence on it.

FIGURE 4-2 Typical Project Stakeholders

Internal Stakeholders	External Stakeholders
▪ Sponsor	▪ Competitors
▪ Project Manager	▪ Regulatory Agencies
▪ Functional Managers	▪ Suppliers
▪ Executive Management	▪ Subcontractors
▪ Team Members	▪ Partnering Organizations
▪ Performing Organization	▪ Environmental Groups
	▪ Project Customer

Information Gathering

Once stakeholders have been identified, the project team should gather information about them. Try to determine the strengths and weaknesses of each. Do not try to shortcut this step.

Often, project teams will immediately jump into the analysis of a stakeholder without gathering any intelligence. (This can be particularly troublesome on product development teams that are staffed with engineers. Engineers—this author included—have a habit of wanting to jump right into solution mode without much planning and analysis.) Keep this step as simple as possible but gather as much information as you deem necessary to analyze a stakeholder's interest in your project.

> **TIP:** Do not perform stakeholder identification and analysis in a vacuum. To ensure a comprehensive list, be sure you involve the project team. In addition to providing diversity of insight, the process will help build team cohesion.

Analyzing Interest

This step analyzes the specific stake in the outcome of your project held by each person or group. Ask this question: Assuming the project is successful, will it have a positive or negative impact on this stakeholder? Obviously, a stakeholder with much to lose from a successful project will be a project opponent. If the stakeholder expects significant gain, you have a proponent.

The interests of each stakeholder should be compared to the others. This will bring to light some of the competing interests that will undoubtedly exist on your project, and you will need all of your negotiation and bargaining skills to reconcile them. Bargaining and negotiation are the two defining elements of organizational politics.[2] (In Chapter 6, we will discuss the skill of negotiation and offer several techniques to aid you in managing competing stakeholder expectations and interests.)

Another way to analyze stakeholders is to consider whether they are positive or negative (allies or adversaries). This can be done by identifying individuals or groups who do not want your project to succeed—potential project saboteurs. This dynamic can make the political environment truly precarious.

For example, consider executive management as a stakeholder group. While a particular executive may want the project to be successful, if that executive is in operations, for example, and your project goal is to find alternative sources of cheaper manufacturing, another executive may not support the project because it runs counter to a particular agenda and priorities. In such situations, when there are toes stepped on, there's great potential for conflict and political maneuvering.

This process of identifying and analyzing stakeholder interest may be needed throughout the entire project. If this is the case, repeat the stakeholder management process as necessary.

Determining Proximity

Proximity refers to how close a stakeholder is to the ongoing work of the project. A stakeholder who is involved in day-to-day project activities and tasks has proximity to the project. Likewise, a project team member has proximity. On the other hand, other project stakeholders will be distant, as is the case

Keep at It

Stakeholder identification and analysis is an iterative process that should be performed throughout the project lifecycle. As a project progresses, different stakeholder groups may be identified while others may recede or even disappear.

with competitors and most suppliers. Proximity may be an indicator of a stakeholder's interest and potential ability to influence other stakeholders.

Assessing Influence

Some project stakeholders will have the power to strongly influence or even to terminate a project. The project sponsor and customer certainly have this authority. The majority of stakeholders cannot terminate a project, but they may be able to influence its key decisions, direction, or outcomes. The stakeholder identification process, coupled with a good understanding of your project's culture and environment, will provide the insights you need to identify those stakeholders with influence.

Let's assume that you're managing the construction of a sewage treatment plant. Stakeholder groups external to the performing organization have the influence to terminate the project outright. For example, regulatory agencies and environmental and political watchdog groups can have significant influence. The regulatory agency can refuse to grant the needed permits; the environmentalists may stage demonstrations and arouse public opposition to the plant.

When assessing the influence of stakeholders, consider how their influence may reach across project boundaries to other stakeholders. If a stakeholder has minimal direct influence on the project but has significant influence over a constituent project stakeholder that holds direct power, that stakeholder should be identified as having a high level of influence by proximity.

A useful tool assessing influence is a strength, weakness, opportunity, and threat (SWOT) analysis. In the interest of time and competing demands, it may be possible to perform a SWOT analysis only on the stakeholders that have the greatest impact on a project's outcome. Time will certainly not permit this analysis to be performed in any significant detail for every project stakeholder.

It's not necessarily the output of the stakeholder SWOT analysis that is most important. Rather, it's the process of identifying the stakeholders, discussing how they interrelate, and determining how they may impact the project that provides the most value.

Developing Strategies

After identifying stakeholder strengths and weaknesses, identify your opportunities to engage them. Also determine what they may perceive as a threat to their interests. If the stakeholder is a project proponent, consider ways to make maximize use of their strengths and minimize their weaknesses. While formulating this strategy, leverage their opportunity to help you and minimize the threat they pose. If the stakeholder is an opponent of the project, consider how to play their strengths into your hand for the good of your project while also considering their weaknesses. You should also develop contingency plans to countermove their strengths while playing against their identified weaknesses.

TIP: It's not easy to identify and assess the strengths and weaknesses of others. This process will be subjective at best if it's done with regard to personality. Instead, work with the project team and peers to assess their behavior. Consider how the stakeholder has behaved and the decisions they've made in past situations. This is the best way to create as objective an assessment as possible.

Predicting Behavior

When key project deliverable dates draw near, how will a client respond to a milestone slip of one week? How will functional managers respond when a project team requires the team members for an additional period? During execution, will a project sponsor accept a cost overrun of 5 percent?

The answer to these questions is, of course, that it depends—which is the point of stakeholder management. If you have managed stakeholder expectations, surprises may be minimal. Admittedly, identifying how an individual stakeholder or stakeholder group will respond to any given situation is not a perfect science. However, having a sufficient level of knowledge about the stakeholder will allow you to better manage stakeholder expectations and project outcomes. If the stakeholder is relatively removed from the project or you have not worked with them in the past, work hard to see their viewpoint. Understanding their stake in the project outcome will greatly improve your chance of predicting their behavior.

Striking a Balance

As a final note on stakeholder management, recognize that keeping all stakeholders satisfied is simply not possible—nor is it practical. If the customer is entirely happy with the price of the project, the project sponsor is likely to be unhappy with the profit margins. Likewise, if a customer is satisfied with a project manager's willingness to accept project changes, the team will more than likely be angered by the inability of the project manager to freeze requirements and control scope. The project team must expect some change in requirements from the client because their needs typically become more clear and defined as the project progresses. Likewise, the client must not expect every change to be accepted without question. To do so would not be in the best interest of the project or the client.

After a stakeholder analysis has been performed, realize that it's also not practical to manage every identified stakeholder. Much like sorting out the most critical patients in a hospital emergency room, you have to perform a sort of triage for stakeholders. Those with a high potential to impact the project should be managed, and others should be monitored. If, in a subsequent analysis, a stakeholder's position changes significantly, they should be moved from a monitored to a managed state.

Mapping Stakeholders

The project manager has many tools at his or her disposal to aid in the mapping of project stakeholders. My preference is a simple spreadsheet. I can sort the spreadsheet based on priority, proximity, influence, or virtually any other category I deem necessary to a given project. Figure 4-3 is a sample stakeholder map formatted in a spreadsheet.

For this particular map, the project team is beginning the development of a project and has been through the identification process outlined in Figure 4-1. This table now attempts to map the stakeholders identified. For the sake of brevity, I've included only a few of the myriad project stakeholders that would normally be identified as part of the process. You can use this stakeholder map to plan communications, manage relationships, or develop a more encompassing political and conflict management strategy (discussed in Chapter 8).

Because the human mind tends to process images better than text, a new method of stakeholder mapping, The *Stakeholder Circle*™, has been developed to represent stakeholder influence and proximity with concentric circles and color coding to quickly and easily identify a project's stakeholder profile.[3] The

FIGURE 4-3 Sample Stakeholder Map

Stakeholder or Group	Influence Impact (High/ Med/Low)	Proximity (Near/ Mid/Far)	Influence (Direct/ Indirect)	Project Termination Authority (Y/N)	May Influence (Stakeholder)	General Information
Project Sponsor	High	Mid	Direct	Y	All Stakeholders	This stakeholder has a vested high interest in the project, but is usually not involved in day-to-day operations. The sponsor has the power to terminate the project.
Customer	High	Near	Direct	Y	All Stakeholders	The project customer has a very high interest in the project with near proximity as communication is occurring on a daily basis. The customer has the power to terminate the project.
Project Manager	High	Near	Indirect	N	All Stakeholders	On this particular project, the project manager has the typical authority profile of directing but not controlling all resources. However, the project manager has the ability to indirectly influence all stakeholders.
VP, Engineering	High	Mid	Indirect	N	Project Sponsor, Functional Managers	This executive-level stakeholder has a high influence impact because of a professional relationship with the project sponsor. This stakeholder may indirectly influence the project by discussing (on a personal level) project outcomes and priorities with the project sponsor.
Functional Manager #1	Med	Mid	Indirect	N	Team Member, Functional Managers	This functional manager is the manager of a project resource, and thereby has the power to interject conflict between a team member's functional responsibilities and his or her responsibility to the project.

technique is truly ingenious and has been developed through sound research design.

KEY POINTS

■ Managing project stakeholders is a critical task for the project manager. Seeing project objectives from a stakeholder perspective and understanding what each has to gain or lose from a project's success will help in predicting behavior and formulating engagement strategies.

■ Keeping stakeholders updated on project status, problems, and risks will enhance your relationship and help you understand their concerns and views. Communicate with key project stakeholders regularly.

■ The entire stakeholder identification and management process is a team sport. Involve your team members in the process to gather the most diverse set of viewpoints possible.

■ Stakeholders can be project allies or adversaries. They may be internal or external individuals or groups (even competitors), and each may have something to gain or lose by the project being completed.

■ Identifying, assessing, and analyzing stakeholders is a dynamic and repetitive process that should be done throughout the project lifecycle.

TAKE ACTION

■ *Assemble the project team.* Have each member identify and write down the names of four key individuals or groups they feel are project stakeholders. After they've identified the stakeholders, have the team members write what they believe each has to gain or lose from the project. Then have them write one or two strengths and weaknesses by each name. Gather the papers and write the responses on a whiteboard. Identify the similarities, differences, and gaps. Discuss with the team.

■ *Interview members of the project leadership team individually.* Ask each for their views on the project's objectives, schedule, and key milestones. After they've answered, ask them to consider the same questions from the perspective of the project sponsor, the project customer, and upper management. Did the answers change? Why?

■ *From the key stakeholder list, call (do not email) the most critical three stakeholders that are project allies.* Discuss the project with them, asking them how they prefer to be kept informed and how often. Document their responses and schedule stakeholder check-in dates on your calendar.

☐

Endnotes

1. Project Management Institute, *A Guide to the Project Management Body of Knowledge*, 3rd ed. (Newtown Square, PA: Project Management Institute, 2004).
2. Jeffrey K. Pinto, Ph.D., *Power and Politics in Project Management* (Newtown Square, PA: Project Management Institute, 1996).
3. Stakeholder Management Pty Ltd, *Stakeholder Circle*™ (South Melbourne, Australia). The *Stakeholder Circle*™ uses methodology based on the results of research by Dr. Lynda Bourne. For more information about Dr. Bourne's research and the *Stakeholder Circle*™, refer to http://www.stakeholder-management.com.

Sean's World
Keep Them Close

Tuesday at the office passed without incident. Sean spent the afternoon examining the project schedule in hopes of finding a way to fast-track or crash the schedule to recover some time. He spent several hours on the task, and it finally paid off. Sean was able to find a critical path task that could be done in parallel near the end of the project, allowing him to shorten the critical path. He carried a sense of accomplishment with him from the office.

Over the course of their meetings, Mariah had come to realize that Sean was a fine project manager, technically. He'd obviously mastered the art of estimating, scheduling, and several other hard skills of project management. The one major shortcoming she'd identified was his lack of the softer skills, which would really be the element that would tip the success scale in his favor. Mariah had discussed this with him, and he was honest in admitting to her that his people skills were, indeed, the biggest problem he struggled with. She'd offered to teach him some of the many things she'd learned over the course of her career, things that might help him work more effectively with his team and others within the organization.

Sean arrived at The Mud and greeted Mariah. He slid into the booth, inquiring, "What did you want to discuss with me tonight, Mariah?"

"Over the many months left on this project, as I'm sure you've already discovered, you're going to encounter many different people who have varied interests in Sagebrush. Each one of these people is a stakeholder of one form or another. Perhaps they'll have something to gain or, perhaps, something to lose if Sagebrush is a success. How will you manage them, Sean? Have you given any thought to how you'll engage these stakeholders? Do you even know what their interests are in Sagebrush?" she asked.

Sean looked up. "I am aware of many people with something at stake in Sagebrush. But I haven't really thought about how to manage them. What do you suggest?"

"Sean, over the course of my career I discovered that if I didn't manage the major stakeholders, they'd somehow manage me. Taking the time to think about each one paid dividends as a project progressed. I could anticipate reactions better, gauge when there might be conflict, and devise a strategy to deal with each stakeholder."

"I could definitely use that on this project, Mariah. But how do I get started?"

Mariah reached down to the seat to grab a stack of papers, which she handed to Sean. The first sheet had a cycle diagram drawn on it of what appeared to be a process. The remaining sheets had written descriptions of each one of the steps that were in the circles of the diagram. The last sheet contained a table of names with comments. It appeared to be from one of her projects long since past.

"Toward the middle of my career, I began to take notes on the things that I learned so I would be able to refer back to them. Here are some notes I took on how to manage project stakeholders. Let's start with the diagram on the first page. It summarizes the process I used. As you can probably guess, it begins with identifying as many of the major stakeholders that you can think of. This includes people both inside and outside your organization. Let's go through this process, Sean, using one person you can think of who's a stakeholder in your project. Who would you like to choose?"

Sean thought for a moment. "How about Lynn Williams, the marketing lead on my team?"

"Good. Let's use Lynn and work through this process so you'll understand how to proceed. We'll create a sheet for each stakeholder and consolidate it into a table later. I presume Lynn's internal to the company?" asked Mariah jokingly.

"Yes, she is."

Mariah continued, "What do you know about Lynn from your interactions with her? Do you have any thoughts on her objectives, goals, or desires?"

"Well, I do know she's pretty well connected within the company. She's been there over 20 years."

Mariah replied, "That's good, but not what I'm after. As a project manager, I want to know what makes Lynn tick. What is it that she values? Do you have any understanding of these things?"

Sean thought for a moment and said, "Unfortunately, I don't know as much about her as I believe you're looking for."

"That's fine for now, Sean. But try to find out these things about her. Talk to her to see if you can understand her better. This is an ongoing process in the project, so you'll have a chance to update this understanding and document it later. Now, how about her interest in the project? Do you know anything about that? Does she want it to succeed? What does she have to gain or lose?"

"As I understand it, Mariah, BSOD has a policy of compensating marketing as a percentage of sales attained in each person's region. So it's in Lynn's best interest to help Sagebrush succeed."

"Good, Sean. Write that down. Next, we have to identify how close she is to the project. I've heard you say that's she's on your team. Is that correct?"

Sean responded quickly, "Yes, she's one of my core team members."

"Great, that's another data point for us. Now we can get back to your first response. You said that she was 'well-connected' in the company. What did you mean by that?"

Sean took a moment to recall his thought. "I've often seen Lynn speaking to really high executives in the company. In her job, she's often in front of C-level executives to give presentations and prepare them for client engagements. She's been very active in the BSOD leadership club too, which has helped her get in front of senior executives."

"That's good, Sean. We're getting a better picture of Lynn as a stakeholder now. From what you've described, I'd say that Lynn has a direct ability to influence other stakeholders. If you agree, let's record this."

"Explain what you mean by 'direct' influence, Mariah. I'm not real clear on that."

"When I say 'direct' influence, I mean that she has the ability to impact other stakeholders' views and decisions directly, without having to persuade someone else to do it for her. That would be 'indirect' influence—using someone else to do your bidding for you because you're not very connected with them, or because there's a relationship issue involved."

"Thanks, Mariah. That's what I thought," said Sean.

Mariah continued her questioning. "Now that we have a better understanding of who Lynn is as a stakeholder in the Sagebrush project, let's strategize how we can best work with her on the project. Any thoughts, Sean?"

"If I look at what I wrote down thus far, Mariah, I can see that she's very interested since she has a high stake in the project, is very close to the execution of the project, and has the ability to directly influence other important stakeholders."

"Good. So what do you think you should do as it relates to Lynn, the project, and the daily workings on your project team?"

"I should definitely use her influence."

"True, but what else, Sean? What should you do every day to help build or improve a relationship with her to aid the success of your project?" asked Mariah.

"Keep her informed and involved?"

Mariah responded immediately. "That's exactly right, Sean. If you keep her well-informed and tied to the major decisions and workings of the project on a daily basis, she'll be more apt to see you as an ally and be more willing to help you. Then, as you come to know her better, you'll be able to gauge how she'll respond in any given situation and how her influence may be used to better position the project."

"But, isn't that manipulation? It sounds very unethical, like I'm 'using' the relationship for personal gain."

"Sean, I realize that it may seem like that as we sit here and do the analysis. But all we're doing is trying to understand these stakeholders better from a professional standpoint. As you go through this process and time progresses, you'll have a better understanding of them as people and not simply resources. You'll be able to build better relationships, leverage their strengths to overcome your weaknesses, and position everyone for success in the long run."

"When you put it that way, it does make more sense, Mariah."

Mariah added, "You'll also be able to communicate with them better because you understand them better. In the meantime, over the rest of the week, fill out these sheets for each project core team member, your sponsor, and any other major stakeholder you can think of. If you don't have all the information, ask others who may have it. When you have this done, put everything in a table like the one on the last page of the handout I gave you. You'll be able to get the information at a glance for everyone at one time, and you can use it to make quick decisions or consider actions and next steps that may need to occur prior to engaging someone for help."

"Thanks Mariah, I'm looking forward to seeing you next week already."

Communication

If there is one indispensable skill that a project manager must possess, it's communication. As a project manager, you can expect to spend as much as 90 percent of your time engaged in communication during the lifecycle of a particular project. Poor communication is one of the primary contributors to conflict in project management. If their communication skills are weak, project managers increase the probability that unclear goals and task requirements will be relayed to project team members. Additionally, there is a greater likelihood of interpersonal conflict, which can ripple throughout your project team and lead to late delivery, missed milestones, and reduced team cohesion. Project managers must also possess the ability to communicate flawlessly when negotiating in highly political situations, when failure to communicate can have disastrous results.

The multitude of communication modes and media available to us is both a blessing and a curse. On one hand, information is readily available, easily accessible, and provided through a multitude of media. On the other hand, we face an over-whelming amount of information that we must sort through and make sense of every day. Communication is truly the key-stone of project management and can be considered one of the deciding factors determining project success.

Communication Modes

On the surface, communication appears to be a simple con-cept. Only three elements are required—a sender, a channel by which to transmit the message, and a receiver. However, a myriad of errors can occur at any point in the process—errors that lead to missed, minimized, or unclear communication.

Communication is not one-way. Consider a simple con-versation between two people: The message is encoded by the sender, processed, and translated into words to be sent through the channel. The message is sent, and the receiver sends back a signal (e.g., a nod, a grimace) that the transmis-sion has been received (or not). Once received, the message goes to the brain of the receiver to be decoded and processed. All the while, interpretations and impressions occur. On the whole, interpersonal communication is a complex process, which is why it is inherently so difficult.

Consider also that each individual does not typically receive a communicated message in a truly pristine state. That is, per-sonal ideologies and filters are applied to the message both when transmitted and when received. These may be experi-

> **"I Heard What You Said, But. . . ."**
>
> It's possible for a message to be decoded incorrectly based on the receiver's background and personal experiences. Moreover, the sender may not even realize that the message could be understood in the way the receiver, processing it through his or her own filters, may translate it. Always be mindful of this possibility when communicating. Check for understanding.

enced in many different forms, including facial expressions, body posture, and vocal tone.

We'll now take a closer look at three main modes of communication—verbal, visual, and written.

Verbal

When communicating verbally, we encode thoughts and ideas into spoken words. In addition to simply sending the words, we give modulation to our voice, which adds meaning to the message. We vary the volume and tone of our voice, and may also pace our speaking in a slow or fast manner. By doing these things, we try to ensure our messages are received with the purpose intended. For example, we may display anger not only by the words we choose to speak, but also by raising our volume and tone. These aids can be a means of implying or asserting power, authority, agreement, or any number of other possibilities.

Visual

We also communicate through the use of nonverbal visual cues—our body language. If we're angry we may also shake

TIP: Sixty-five to 90 percent of all interpersonal communication is interpreted through body language.[1] If your body is sending a different message than your mouth, the chances of an incorrect interpretation are immense. These miscommunications can lead directly to conflict or political positioning.

our fist, for example. But this nonverbal communication mode is usually performed at the subconscious level. In any typical setting, it can be used as an aid to interpersonal communication if we're aware of its many subtleties.

If the person we're talking to rolls their eyes, it's obvious that they are not in alignment with us. However, other forms of visual feedback are not so obvious. As project managers, when we're in meetings we are often the ones leading and doing most of the communicating. We may get so involved with the message that we lose touch with the visual feedback. Why is he staring out the window? Why is she doodling? If only we'd pay more attention.

We also use visual communication when we speak. We can use our hands to make a point, our facial expressions to relay emotion, and our posture to communicate our level of energy or excitement. Effectively communicating requires us to use all the tools available to us to make sure we're understood.

Eye contact is crucial. Some say you should maintain eye contact two-thirds of the time when communicating in a business settings, and 80 percent of the time in intimate relationships.[2] When maintaining eye contact, a steady gaze into the eyes is not required. Focus on the triangle formed by the eyes and the nose of the receiver. Remember too that eye contact is culture-specific. In the Japanese culture, for example, people are not accustomed to long periods of eye contact and will become uncomfortable. If you sense that you're causing distress by your level of eye contact, minimize its use to ease the situation and enhance the communication.

Written

Written communication, both formal and informal, is used extensively in the business environment. To a project manager, written communication is one of the requisite modes for documenting project decisions, contractual agreements, and project plans. Unfortunately, one of the most common forms of written communication used today is email. Don't get me wrong, email is great for communicating quickly; however, it's become second nature for us. I've seen many project managers get caught in a political firestorm or conflict because a message was sent too quickly and without forethought. Information that is conveyed in email contains a wealth of opportunities for misinterpretation.

Written communication may contain passages that can be interpreted as innuendo, sarcasm, or as having hidden meaning or agenda. Beware when communicating in writing that your message may be construed in a less-than-ideal manner. As a general rule, write your message and read it several times before sending it. This is especially true of critical documents and email messages. If in doubt, have someone else read your message and ask for their interpretation. Also try to keep written communication as succinct as possible. Writing two paragraphs where only one or two sentences would have sufficed will elicit either boredom or angst in your reader.

Barriers to Communication

We do not transmit and receive messages in a pure or pristine state. This is an aspect of communicating that makes interpersonal communication so challenging. When we communicate, we process the message through our personal filters, and then the receiver processes it again through his or her own filters. These filters are the byproduct of our past experiences, cultures, and values, and they can be barriers to communication. Let's look at some of the more common communication barriers encountered within a typical project management setting, including interpretation, interpersonal style differences, and cultural differences.

Interpretation

As we all well know, a message may be taken out of context. In a project environment, we are often communicating issues, risks, action items, and many other items that are open to interpretation. When you send a communication, whether written or spoken, you often communicate your belief—not the fact or intent. Suppose one of your team member sends a message that says "the existence of a particular software defect *may* drive additional software releases, resulting in increased project cost of $25,000 related to development and test activities." What you may actually hear (interpret) is "this defect *will* cost us $25,000." The sender must ensure that the receiver has decoded the message correctly and inferred the proper meaning.

TIP: Your speed of thought is much greater than the pace of your speech. Because of this, our minds begin to wander when not actively engaged in the moment. Thus, listening can be a difficult task. The gaps of time spent while processing speech can easily be filled by wandering and daydreaming. When you are the one communicating, remember this and ask for confirmation of understanding as you converse. When listening, communicate your interpretation of the message and ask for agreement and clarification.

In many instances, interpretation mistakes may simply be attributed to not paying close enough attention to the message and not reading it, or rereading it, carefully. Perhaps your team member embedded the message about the $25,000 cost increase within a long e-mail of several paragraphs that included a request to take next week off. And perhaps as you read it you got bored or distracted and let your mind wander momentarily, losing the meaning of the message.

Interpersonal Style Differences

A personality clash between team members is one of the most common communication problems you can face as the leader of a project team. It usually stems from past animosity or severe personality differences, and is a difficult communication barrier to overcome. If project team members have had difficulties on past projects, chances are high that these differences will be carried forward and surface on your project. The parties in question may simply choose not to communicate with each other and avoid any and all potential contact with one another.

Even if team members have not had past problems, differences in individual personalities are common enough that they're certain to exist on a project team. This is especially true of large teams. Author Tim Sanders speaks of how a person's "likeability" determines much of the success they experience in all aspects of their lives.[3] A person's likeability is also a contributor to interpersonal differences. If we perceive someone to be difficult to work with, we may automatically be unwilling to accept their message or its meaning. This is especially true if their core values and beliefs are in direct opposition to our own.

Think about a particularly challenging colleague you've worked with in the past. What was it that really got under your skin? If this person had an idea or thought, were you ever inclined to reject it initially, even if it was a great one? Would you intentionally find fault or oppose the idea just on the principle that you would not let this person get by with an idea (even a good one) so easily when they challenged you actively? This mindset reflects a difficult—and common—challenge in interpersonal communications.

Cultural Differences

In today's global business environment, cultural awareness and sensitivity are required for effective communication. Even if the project you're currently working on does not reach across international borders, chances are that you have many cultures represented on your team. Not understanding the subtleties in cultural norms can increase the chance of misunderstandings and communication gaps. Culture is usually referred to in terms of nationality, but it is defined by much more than a country of origin. In essence, culture is a "historically transmitted pattern of meanings embodied in symbols."[4]

Culture has two aspects, the visible and the invisible, and can be compared to an iceberg. What we see on the surface as cultural differences—such as architecture, cars, music, and fashion—represent only the tip of the iceberg protruding from the water's surface. The aspects of culture that most affect communication, such as attitudes, behaviors, and beliefs, lie below the surface and are more difficult to perceive. Yet they have the most impact on communications.

Several cultural challenges are common in project management. Some of these are evident in vendor relations, meeting styles, problem resolution, negotiation styles, leader and subordinate relationships and interactions, and ethics standards. To overcome some of these challenges we must do two things. First, we must understand the cultural backgrounds of others on our project teams. Second, we must understand our own cultural style.[5] If you achieve these two things, you will greatly increase your understanding of the potential cultural gaps on the project team. When you've identified these gaps, you'll become more mindful of the other person's cultural style and be able to predict situations that may cause difficulty.

The Path to Effective Communication

As project managers, how do we overcome these barriers? Certain techniques can help you overcome some of the more challenging communication issues we all face as project managers, including an awareness of perceptions and personal filters, and active listening.

Perception and Physiological Response Awareness

The popular author C. S. Lewis once said, "What you see and hear depends a great deal on where you're standing." In other words, your perceptions are shaped by your background. Your beliefs, values, culture, and history all play an active part in shaping your thoughts, ideas, and opinions. And most important for us here, they influence how you receive and interpret messages from other people.

Let's suppose that someone has just made a recommendation you

TIP: When listening, be "care-full." Listening when you are aware of cultural or personality differences and having empathy for the other party will allow you to reach a common intersection with the communicator. Focus on the person communicating to help communication flow smoother.

perceive as far-fetched, and maybe that individual is someone you've had difficulties with in the past. To a certain extent, your reactions will always depend on the individuals involved, what is said, and whether you have direct relationships with those individuals. But are you questioning the suggestion's outlandishness because of your impression of the individual making it? Most project managers would probably not even raise questions about such a reaction, which amounts to many missed opportunities for true communication.

What is it that stops us from making effective use of these opportunities to seek true understanding with others? It takes a lot of work to carefully clarify and question to bring us to true alignment, while it takes virtually no effort to form an instant opinion based on our set assumptions. This gap between opinion and understanding explains a lot of miscommunication and frustration.[6]

An animal can call upon several strategies when confronted with danger. Some of the more common defenses are withdrawing to escape the danger (flee), becoming immobile until the danger passes (freeze), striking back to ward off the danger (fight), and submitting (give in to the other party). We have similar responses to danger programmed into our very being. Our response to social threats can be exactly the same. For example, in a social setting, we may unexpectedly be challenged by a senior member of the team. At this moment, a physiological response occurs in the brain that causes you to instinctively fight, freeze, flee, or submit. In organizations this translates into vocally defending one's position, withdrawing, becoming passive, or giving in to demands.

As a project manager, I've learned that it takes considerable vigilance and focus to understand how to respond in a better way and not to react automatically. If we understand our natural response to certain situations and are aware of how we naturally react, we can counteract the effect and move toward common understanding. Understanding always-present personal filters can enable us to take this approach.

Personal Filter Awareness

Our personal filters—shaped by our past experiences, education, culture, and assumptions—cause us to subconsciously frame transmitted or received messages. Ultimately, the outputs of these filters become our perceptions of reality—and the source of a lot of misunderstanding, miscommunication, and conflict.

Our fixed perceptions generally cloud our understanding (although in rare instances they can enhance it). Our filters and our perceptions are a mark of our unique individuality. Thus, you might find someone very annoying and difficult to work with while others do not. An individual may demonstrate traits that you have difficulty getting past. Someone who talks loudly or fast might remind you of someone from your past, for example. And your thoughts and interactions might become clouded by that automatic response.

As well as having filters that affect our perceptions of others, we also have filters that shape our interactions with others. Suppose someone has just asked for help on a task that would take you three hours to do. But you have your own task to complete, one that is on a deadline. Many of us have been brought up to believe that it's best to help others because "what goes around comes around." You may have a response filter that is shaped by your desire to be seen by others as helpful. Thus, you accept the task and put yours aside. Because you've delayed your own work, you may get into trouble with your boss. As a result of your response filter, which has been shaped by many past influences, you've now put yourself at risk.[7]

Once we are aware of our personal filters, our next job is to overcome them. This is not a trivial task. These filters have been built through many years of personal experiences and are active in our subconscious. When we employ them, we usually don't do it consciously. However, this is exactly what we must be do—bring them out of the realm of the automatic subconscious—if we are to overcome them.

Take care to notice the instinctual responses you have while communicating. You may notice an emotional, physiological, or psychological effect. Use this awareness to help you understand how you throw up automatic barriers. Remember that your perception is the result of communicated messages being sifted through your emotional filters. One way to overcome that barrier is to use active listening.

Active Listening

One of the most useful—yet underutilized—tools in our communications toolbox is active listening. It is especially useful in situations of confrontation and conflict. Humans spend a lot of time formulating a response to communication as it is being received rather than focusing on understanding the

There are two primary components to communication, content and feeling. Content is what is being said and feeling is how it is being said. *How* something is being said is the major contributor to understanding *what* is being said. Any parent can relate to this directly.

message that's being communicated. Active listening is exactly that—active. Rather than listening to the message and assuming that you understand it, ask clarifying questions to check your understanding. It's useful to echo your understanding of the message to the other party. Restating key points to affirm your understanding (or your misunderstanding) will help you gain a clearer comprehension and build dialogue.

Active listening is about "being here now." Do not allow yourself to become distracted while you are engaged in a conversation. Checking email and typing documents while taking a phone call is not being here now—and it's downright rude. Do not assume that you already understand what's being communicated. Doing so will provide the temptation to shut down your listening. Rather, listen intently with caring and empathy. It's a key trait of a successful project leader.

Another way of actively listening is to give feedback. This feedback will assist the communicator in making corrections to the way the message is being sent. It may also serve to reinforce their communication if you indeed do understand the message. Nonverbal cues such as eye contact and body posture can relay attentiveness and understanding.

Finally, it's important to note that members of our project teams want us to be there for them. Occasionally, a team member simply needs you to be available to listen to them while they share their concerns and thoughts. People do not always want you to solve their issues. They may simply want an empathetic ear to hear them out and be nonjudgmental. Make yourself available and open to them. If you do, you'll be well on your way to being a caring leader whom people will willingly follow.

KEY POINTS

■ Communication is one of the most important duties of a project manager. Ninety percent of the project manager's time may be spent in communication.

■ There are three major categories of communication—verbal, visual, and written. The majority of the information in a spoken message is transmitted via body language and tone of voice.

■ Various barriers to communication exist. Cultural variations, interpersonal differences, and literal interpretation are a few of the more common barriers that a project manager must overcome to communicate effectively.

■ Physiological response to communication is as evident in social settings as it is in situations of physical danger. The natural response to fight, fly, freeze, or submit is ingrained in each of us and represents our way of responding to danger on a subconscious level. Becoming aware of our natural reaction can disarm this response mechanism and move us on the path toward effective communication.

■ Active listening increases the chance of successful communication because it enables you to confirm your understanding.

TAKE ACTION

■ *When listening, keep your mind open.* With the next person you communicate with, pay particular attention to what they're saying. Really focus on understanding the meaning of what they're trying to say. Do not form a response while you are listening to them. Empty your thoughts and give them your attention. Maintain eye contact and ask clarifying questions to check your understanding. How difficult was it to focus without letting your mind wander?

■ *Practice active listening.* Gather your project team and split them into teams of two or three persons. Ask each team to write illogical sentences on pieces of paper, like "We love to eat mud with our spaghetti." Have one person from each team go to the front of the room with their written, illogical sentence and give them a discussion topic or just engage them in casual conversation. Their object in the course of conversation is to slip in the illogical sentence without the other teams realizing it. Of the other teams listening to the speaker, the team with the most correct guesses at the hidden sentence wins. The exercise builds team cohesion, illustrates what it's like to be truly engaged in communication, and is FUN.

■ *Work to communicate not by focusing on your own understanding of a message, but by focusing on how the other party will best understand.* Break your project team into pairs and ask each person in the pair to choose a topic. Ask them to consider how they would expect the other person to communicate key points of that topic, and tell them to write their thoughts down separately. Then ask them to engage in conversation about each other's topics. Did they receive the communication as expected? Ask them to compare their actual conversations with their prior thoughts (separately written down earlier), and to discuss these comparisons with each other and as a team.

☐

Endnotes

1. Anne Warfield, *Your Body Speaks Volumes, But Do You Know What It's Saying?* http://www.hodu.com/body-language.shtml (accessed July 8, 2007).
2. Kevin Hogan, Ph.D., *Talk Your Way to the Top: Communication Secrets to Change Your Life* (Gretna, LA: Pelican Publishing, 2000).
3. Tim Sanders, *The Likeability Factor: How to Boost Your L-Factor and Achieve Your Life's Dreams* (New York: Three Rivers Press, 2005).
4. Earnest Gundling, *Working GlobeSmart: 12 People Skills for Doing Business Across Borders* (Palo Alto, CA: Davies-Black Publishing, 2003).
5. One of the more useful tools for exploring your cultural style is the *Peterson Cultural Style Indicator*™ (Saint Paul, MN: Across Cultures, LLC). Access it online at http://www.acrosscultures.com.
6. Mickey Connolly and Richard Rianoshek, Ph.D., *The Communication Catalyst: The Fast (But Not Stupid) Track to Values for Customers, Investors, and Employees* (Chicago: Dearborn Trade Publishing, 2002).
7. In his book *Powerful Project Leadership* (Vienna, VA: Management Concepts, 2002), Wayne Strider lists many examples of personal filters that shape our behaviors and communications. I highly recommend this book as a great resource for anyone seeking to investigate overall leadership as it pertains to project management.

Sean's World
Communication
and Spaghetti

"Sean, communication is not a spectator sport. True communication takes active involvement."

The particularly warm and inviting Monday evening found Sean and Mariah taking a break from their ordinary meeting place in the coffee shop, opting instead to walk the Sixteenth Street Mall. They stopped at a crosswalk to wait for the light to beckon them safely across.

"I *was* actively participating, Mariah. I was very clear in my direction."

Mariah turned to face Sean, "That's the funny thing about communication Sean: It's not like the mail. What you send is not always what's received."

Sean pondered what she'd said. It struck him profoundly. "Well, I suppose you could look at it that way."

"If you want to engage in true communication, I mean *real* and *honest* communication, you need to always be aware. You see, it's only partially the other person's job to understand. You also have an obligation to ensure your message came across as you meant it to."

"And how do I accomplish that?"

"Well, let's think about it for a moment, Sean. One of the first things I'll suggest is to look at the person you're communicating with. Really focus to observe. Watch the reaction to what you're saying. You can receive valuable feedback from someone just by observing their behavior and reaction to what you are saying."

As they reached the far sidewalk, Mariah continued. "Take the time to observe. You will be able to pick up some subtle cues about your message. We already do this subconsciously. For example, what does it say to you if I do this when you're speaking to me . . .?" Mariah crossed her arms, rolled her eyes, and looked away.

"I get the impression you're thinking I'm out of my mind."

"That's right, Sean. Well, not that you *are* out of your mind but that the gestures convey the message that I don't quite agree with what you're saying. Then you should question me about my understanding and compare my responses to what your intent was."

He looked at Mariah, puzzled once again. "Question them? If I just told someone something, why would I want to question them?"

"Because you want to be sure they understood your intent," she replied. "Let's try something. Just humor me for a minute."

The two stopped on the sidewalk and Mariah pointed to a hotdog vendor, "Sean, what's that?"

"That's a hotdog stand."

"That's right," said Mariah. She continued, "What am I pointing to that's silver?"

Sean looked and responded, "The cart."

"Now what am I pointing to that's fabric?"

"The canopy."

"That's precisely correct. Did you see that I was always pointing in the same direction, but the things you saw changed with each question I asked? Questioning someone works the same way, Sean. If you take time to read the language their body is speaking and ask questions to test understanding, you'll be well on your way to meaningful communication."

Sean and Mariah crossed the street again and walked back on the opposite side of the mall.

Mariah continued, "I know that when I was a project manager, communication was one of the primary tasks that I performed. I haven't been a project manager for quite some time now, but I can only assume it's even truer now."

"You can say that again, Mariah. It's very difficult to keep up with everything. Just when I sit down to read my email, the phone will ring. While I'm speaking on the phone, someone will page me. Then, I may even have someone walk into my office. The list goes on."

Mariah sighed deeply. "I'm sure glad we didn't have to worry about all of that when I was working. I had a hard enough time keeping up as it was. I can't imagine what you go through these days. One thing I will say is that with all that overload of information, there are certainly more opportunities for misunderstandings and communication gaps now than there ever were. Then again, that means there are also more opportunities for honest and meaningful communication than there ever were."

"Email seems especially tricky, though, because you lose all that body language that we're so dependent on in our communication. There may also be a tendency to hide behind email—you know, like a person experiencing road rage feels safe in the security of their car. I think it may be easier to say something in email you'll regret later than if you were communicating face-to-face with someone."

"I've certainly done that," Sean replied.

"I want to discuss one more thing before we end tonight, Sean."

"What's that?"

"Let's discuss the other side of the coin, Sean—listening. We usually spend far too much time speaking and not nearly enough time listening. I know it sounds like a cliché, but we do have two ears and one mouth for a reason. We should be listening twice as much as speaking. And, I'm not talking about simply listening to what someone's saying, Sean. I'm talking about active listening."

"What's the difference?"

"Listening is passive, Sean. It takes very little effort. In fact, we often find the effort to listen effectively very difficult to muster. We actually get bored if we listen passively. If we listen passively, our minds can wander very easily. Sometimes, we're not listening at all. Instead, we're formulating what we're going to say when it's our turn."

She continued, "Active listening is hard work requiring conscious attention. But if we can do it, we get a reward—increased understanding, accelerated personal growth, and better relationships."

"So, what you're telling me is that because our minds get bored we can essentially 'tune out' the speaker?"

"Exactly, Sean. By the way, that was a good use of active listening on your part."

"How was that active listening?" he asked.

"One of the best practices of active listening is to repeat your understanding of what is being said. This gives the speaker a feedback mechanism to help them know if they're getting their message across."

"There's one more aspect to active listening I'd like to mention, Sean. That's the notion that when we listen actively, we listen not only to what's being said, but what's not being said. I mean body language and tone of voice. Listen carefully when someone's speaking and you'll hear different tones to reflect their mood. Their posture will indicate how engaged they are in the conversation. Someone can be telling you one thing with their voice and yet another with their body language."

The conversation turned to an issue Sean was having at BSOD that he would have to correct before the end of the week. His primary software developer, Shafik Arad, had been removed from the project to work on an upgrade to the current customer relationship management (CRM) application, which had been developed in-house at BSOD. The removal of this key team member was truly alarming, for Sagebrush was in the middle of the software development phase. This key piece of the project would be delayed if the software development was not completed.

"I don't know what I'm going to do about this, Mariah," Sean stated with obvious concern.

"It sounds like you've got some negotiating to do," she replied.

"Yes, I certainly do."

"It's a good thing we discussed communication this evening. Negotiating is all about influence and communication. If you need any help, you can contact me anytime."

"Thanks, Mariah, but I think I'll try this one on my own first, and we'll see what happens."

"Sounds good. I hope it goes well."

Negotiation

Project managers usually do not have formal authority. In the matrix environment most projects are conducted in, the project manager lacks the ability to influence through the positional power of a formal hierarchical structure since team members report back to their own functional (or department) managers. Thus, project managers must rely on other methods. Negotiating skill is one of the tools project managers have at their disposal to help them have influence in this environment.

Negotiation is something we all do every day. Some of us do it knowingly, others unknowingly. As project managers, we negotiate with stakeholders on schedule dates, with resource managers for personnel, and with sponsors for funding. We also negotiate with customers, external agencies, and suppliers. (And, of course, we negotiate with our children, spouses, and others in our personal lives.) With so many negotiations occurring at any given time and in a variety of situations, we must be skilled in the practice and process of negotiation to increase our effectiveness as project managers.

The Need to Negotiate

Leadership, team building, political savvy, conflict management, and communication are among the skills a project manager is required to possess and continually improve. Negotiation is used in each of these areas. Virtually every transaction performed in managing a project is a negotiation of one sort or another.

Early in my engineering career I mistakenly thought that negotiation only took place when a sale was being made. Why, I wondered, should I focus on building negotiating skills when I'm not involved in sales? How naïve I was. Negotiation is important not only in purchases and contracts, but also in work schedules, change management, risk management, and personnel tasking, as well as a myriad of other project activities. An important part of any successful project is the removal of obstacles confronting the project team. Undoubtedly, the project manager will be required to negotiate at some point to facilitate the removal of these obstacles.

Consider this scenario: You have a fast-approaching milestone in your project. A project team member who is key to meeting the milestone has just been reassigned to what corporate headquarters has deemed a higher priority—to help solve a problem with one of the company's current products in the field. This is a common occurrence in many organizations due to limited resources and corporate downsizing. As the project manager, you'll first need to identify the skills required to replace that person. Then you'll have to negotiate with a resource manager to have a person with those skills assigned to the team; failure to do so could result in missing that milestone. If customer payment or incentive is tied to the milestone, your job becomes even more urgent, upping the ante and increasing the pressure to achieve a successful outcome.

Many of us approach negotiations with trepidation and anxiety. This is because we typically approach negotiations in the same way we approach and manage conflict.[1] Studies have shown that without considerable planning, our natural inclination to negotiations follows our conflict style.[2] Look back to Figure 3-1 in Chapter 3, where conflict resolution modes are illustrated. Where do you fit on that map? If you are an accommodator in conflict, you'll typically deal with negotiations the same way. Similarly, if you are a competitor in conflicts, your natural tendency will be to compete in negotiations. When negotiations are imminent, you must understand your natural tendencies and work to adapt your style to the specific situation.

The negotiating situations a project manager will face are usually related to limited resources (personnel and budget), schedule and time constraints, and quality. However, there's another negotiating task that is sometimes overlooked by even experienced project managers—

> **TIP:** Feeling emotional in negotiations is natural. To feel emotion is to be human, especially when the stakes are high. The problems arise when we are not aware of our emotions and instinct takes over. To negotiate in extreme pressure and high-stakes situations, you must control your emotions. If need be, excuse yourself from the negotiation momentarily to gather your composure and recognize the emotions you're feeling. Simply blocking the natural urge to react is often enough to overcome the inherent dangers.

customer expectations. Ensuring that the project customer has reasonable expectations about the outcome of the project is a crucial step in ensuring success.

Negotiation Considerations

Occasionally, we are thrust into a situation requiring negotiations—for example, when a conflict suddenly arises in a meeting. Consider your inclinations as a negotiator and then quickly decide how they should be applied to this conflict. The key is spending time beforehand to reflect on your tendencies so you can apply them appropriately when needed. If you understand yourself, you'll always be prepared for negotiations as the need arises.

Ideally you'll have some time to think things through. But even if a negotiation arises on the spur of the moment, before entering into it, consider the situation and the relative power you hold with respect to the other negotiating party. (If you've done a thorough job of identifying stakeholders' interests and positions, as we discussed in Chapter 4, you'll have this information ready.) Equal power must exist to ensure amicable outcomes. If one party has significantly more power than the other, you're really in more of a compliance situation than a negotiation. Thus, the first requirement for effective negotiation is that both parties are on similar footing. Note that this power need not be formal authority. When you have something critical to the other party, you have significant power to wield.

Another, more obvious, requirement to consider is whether each party has something the other party is interested in. If you have nothing the other party wants or needs, you really have no grounds on which to negotiate.

Another constraint on negotiation is the pressure of time. If the other party discovers that time is one of your constraints (e.g., you need to record a large sales deal prior to fiscal year-end), expect them to delay and use this to their advantage to force you into accepting their terms and conditions. You must guard your external constraints closely so as not to reveal a vulnerability in your position. To be effective, negotiations must operate free and clear from any external pressures.[3]

> **TIP:** Occasionally we have items we consider of low value but that the other side values greatly. These are known as bargaining chips and can be used as a valuable negotiating lever. You may be able to exchange some of your bargaining chips to help you meet your negotiating objective(s). And because you're giving away something of great to value to the other side, you'll begin to build a good-faith relationship and will increase your odds of getting something of value to you later on.

Trust is also a critical aspect of negotiation. Do you trust the other party involved in the negotiation? Have you dealt with them in the past? If so, have they kept their word and agreements? Do they play hardball? It is important to know if you can realistically sit across from someone in a negotiation and believe they're being forthcoming and honest with you. If you do not trust the other party, you'll be much less likely to be open and honest with them, and the negotiation will likely suffer for both parties.

Preparing for Negotiations

As any good project manager knows, planning is the meat-and-potatoes of project execution. Likewise, planning pays dividends in negotiations. But even the best plans never play out exactly as we sketch them out, so you must have a contingency plan—a "plan B," so to speak. To this end, preparing for negotiation involves intelligence gathering, situational awareness, and the ability to build healthy relationships and alliances.

One of the first items to address in negotiating anything is to determine your "best alternative to a negotiated agreement"— or BATNA. This is your fall-back position, the course of action if you're be unable to reach agreement during negotiation. In risk management terms, your BATNA may be thought of as a contingency plan. Ask yourself: "If I'm unable to reach a suitable outcome to this negotiation, what would be my best alternative?" The answer to this question is your BATNA.

When you plan for a negotiation, try to identify the needs and desires of the other party. In doing this, some questions to ponder are: What will my opponent's position be? How will they, or I, open? What are their goals? How can they be persuaded? How can I achieve my goals in this negotiation and still allow them to save face?

TIP: Your BATNA is the course of action you'll take if the negotiation fails. Suppose you are negotiating with a vendor for a lower price on circuit cards. You like working with the vendor, but your budget does not allow the parts to be purchased at the vendor's asking price. If you go into the negotiation with no fall-back position, you may or may not get a price break. However, if you were to get competitive pricing from two or three other vendors, you might be able to get a more attractive price on the circuit cards with your preferred vendor. Other bargaining chips, such as offering future business and a continued relationship with your company, could also be offered.

The answers to these questions can help guide your planning and allow you to ponder strategies you might employ. One of the best ways to approach a negotiation is to agree with the other party on an agenda to guide the process. Often, setting this agenda will require a negotiation in itself. For instance, one negotiator may prefer to address the easier issues first, while another may want to start with the most contentious issues. In either case, setting an agenda ahead of time demonstrates a willingness to work collaboratively and with the other party's interest in mind.

Another consideration in your planning is to foresee possible paths the negotiation may take. Think of this planning as an IF-THEN-ELSE map. For example, *if* they say this, *then* I'll use this reply or strategy, or *else* I'll pursue this path.

My wife used to work as a 911 emergency operator. When the operators receive an emergency phone call, they use a series of flip-cards based on the emergency they're dealing with at the moment. The cards map out responses to the various information they receive from a caller. You may think of mapping your responses in a similar way. Don't go into a negotiation with flip cards, of course. But think about your responses, tactics, and strategies for likely scenarios ahead of time, and you'll be better able to anticipate how to respond in advance of the actual negotiation. When you enter the negotiation, you may have already played through a scenario that arises—giving you a practiced advantage.

As you plan, ask yourself what you want out of the negotiation, what the other party wants out of the negotiation, and at what point you'll be willing to walk away from the negotiation. As you do this, focus on the intersections between your goals and the goals of those across the table from you. Understanding this intersection will help identify strategies that can produce a win-win outcome.

Active Listening and Negotiation

Listening actively is especially important in negotiation. Listening actively does not mean simply trying to internalize what the other party is saying, making assumptions about their statements. It means listening intently, with empathy, and asking clarifying questions to test and refine your assumptions. This may even confirm or cast doubt on a pre-planned tactic for the negotiation while there's still time to adjust it.

Think about a time when you felt you weren't being listened to. Did you feel angry that the other party was simply hearing you out of courtesy instead of being truly engaged in understanding the point you were trying to make? By not being empathetic and listening actively to the other party, you're sending the signal that you do not value their position, which could provoke underhanded tactics and negative emotions in the remainder of the negotiation.

Work at all costs to avoid preconceived notions about the other negotiating party or their position. Ask open-ended, clarifying questions such as, "What I understand you're saying is . . .", or "As I understand it, you're saying . . . can you explain?" While they're replying to your open-ended question, listen to what they're saying, paying particular attention to their meaning and intent.

Emotions and Conflict in Negotiations

Negotiations are performed by human beings with innate desires, agendas, and objectives, so it's reasonable to expect some emotional elements to arise. This is especially true when high stakes are attached to the outcome. Because of the emotion involved in many negotiations, conflict is also to be expected. In fact, depending on the magnitude of what's at stake, negotiation can be an emotionally, mentally, and physically exhausting experience.

Consider a situation in which a worker's union leader is negotiating a new contract with corporate management. These types of negotiations can typically consume weeks or even months before an acceptable agreement can be reached. The stakes are usually very high, and emotions on both sides are intense. Labor contracts often go down to the last minute because until there is the pressure of a deadline—an impending strike, for example—neither side will compromise. In a situation such as this, it's very easy to understand how lengthy negotiations can be both mentally and emotionally challenging.

Some of the conflict we face in negotiation is predictable and some is not. Additionally, while conflict in negotiation is both normal and expected, it can occasionally become so emotionally charged that it escalates to a dysfunctional level.[4] Of course, the definition of "dysfunctional" will vary from negotiator to negotiator. Effective negotiation is not about keeping the lid on things, but about bringing important emotions and considerations to the surface so they may be dealt with quickly and effectively to allow win-win outcomes, if possible.

TIP: In particularly difficult and emotional negotiations, Hollywood talent scout and producer Darrell Kern writes powerful phrases about his emotions and what he wants to accomplish on a white t-shirt he wears under his suit, "On a psychological level, it gives me strength and power over the situation to know what I've written," he says.

In particularly extended and exhausting negotiations, an effective tactic is to allow the opposing side to experience the occasional emotional outburst. Allowing your opponents the opportunity to experience such moments can help pave the way for more reasoned and effective negotiation at a later time.

Winning by Staying Cool

During one negotiation I witnessed, the VP of a business unit tongue-lashed a senior engineering manager. The manager's response was simply to stay calm and explain that he'd done everything he'd been asked to do and that had been agreed upon. The situation strained the relationship, but the VP gained a great deal of respect for the manager and never openly challenged him again. Poise is priceless.

Regardless of the reason for an emotional outburst by your opponent, it's best to contain your own emotions. It can be very tempting to lash out at your opponent to save face. However, doing so will not advance your goal. Avoid this temptation at all costs. Responding emotionally will only increase your chance of failure; emotional negotiation usually leads to ineffective negotiations at best, and failed negotiations at worst. By practicing emotional restraint, you'll display professionalism and actually garner the respect of your negotiation opponent.

KEY POINTS

■ Negotiations occur in every aspect of our personal and professional lives. Being skilled negotiators will serve to benefit our organizations, our projects, and our overall happiness.

■ When engaging other parties, always be prepared to enter into a negotiation. Occasionally, we don't know in advance when we'll be called upon to negotiate.

- Try as much as possible to understand the other negotiating party. Identify their needs, desires, and positions. If possible, find out how they're likely to react in given situations.

- Identify what bargaining chips you have to offer. These figurative chips are of relatively low value to you but are of considerably higher value to the other negotiating party. Offer them to the other negotiating party to help "sweeten the pot" and influence them to concede on other issues.

- Develop your best alternative to a negotiated agreement (BATNA). It's what you'll fall back on should your initial negotiation plans fail.

- Use active listening and ask clarifying questions to enhance communication and trust in a negotiating relationship. There's never a good time to make poor assumptions about another party, but it's especially dangerous in negotiations. Listen with care, empathy, and understanding.

TAKE ACTION

- When negotiating a contract or proposal, *do not be afraid to edit*. Too often, I've seen project managers fall prey to the it's–the-rules trick. The other party defends its language by saying, "This is our standard contract language." I suggest you consider "So what?" as a response in these situations. Follow-up with, "If I'm signing a contract, I will make any changes I deem necessary for the good of my organization and project."

- During your next large negotiation, *let the other party know that the final decision does not rest with you*. Doing so will let the other party know that they need to negotiate with reason and facts—not emotion. If the person they really have to convince is not present, they'll be less likely to use strong emotions to influence others. It will also give you time to think about the offer prior to making a formal decision.

■ *Always ask for more than you expect to get,* because even though you're not likely to get it, you'll at least have room to negotiate. If you're negotiating to sell an item and the other party takes your first price, they are either naïve or you'll wonder what you could have really gotten—or both. In either case, you started out too low.

■ *Practice patience!* Negotiation can be long, grueling, mentally challenging work. Expecting negotiations to be over quickly can lead to leaving too much on the table down the road. Wanting to get it over with and get on with the business at hand is not the most effective way to perform in a negotiation—although it's a fairly common sentiment. Patience and diligence will pay off in the long run.

□

Endnotes

1. G. Richard Shell, *Bargaining for Advantage: Negotiation Strategies for Reasonable People* (New York: Penguin Books, 1999).
2. Ibid.
3. Jeffrey K. Pinto, Ph.D., *Power and Politics in Project Management* (Newtown Square, PA: Project Management Institute, 1996).
4. Kathleen Kelley Reardon, Ph.D., *The Skilled Negotiator: Mastering the Language of Engagement* (San Francisco: Jossey-Bass, 2004).

Sean's World
Train Wreck

It was a rainy Wednesday morning in Denver. Sean hoped the weather inside the building would not match that on the outside—cloudy and ominous. He couldn't help thinking about the task that lay ahead. The lead software developer on Sagebrush, Shafik Arad, was being removed from his project team and reassigned to help work on an upgrade to the company's aging CRM application. Today was Sean's meeting with Tony Chang, Shafik's boss and the manager of the software development resource pool. He would have to state his case with Tony that Shafik should stay with Sagebrush to reduce the risk of the project schedule slipping. Shafik had significant knowledge of the base financial application that was being developed for Sagebrush. Bringing a different developer on at this time would be a very high risk. A significant learning curve would be required before the new developer would be able to contribute at a high level.

Sean finished his early morning tasks of sorting through his email and clearing his voicemail. As the 10:00 a.m. meeting time approached, his pulse quickened and his heart raced. He knew that it would not be easy to convince Tony that Shafik should stay on the project. Sean understood the pressure that Tony was under to provide staff for all the simultaneous projects that were being worked throughout BSOD. He desperately needed to keep Shafik on Sagebrush, but did not like confrontation. Sean knew the meeting would not be easy.

Sean felt uneasy as he opened the door to Tony's office.

"Good morning, Tony," he said.

"Hello, Sean, please have a seat. What can I do for you today?"

Sean sat in the chair directly across from Tony. "Shafik has told me that he's being reassigned to the CRM upgrade project. Is that true?"

"Yes, Sean, it is. Do you have an issue with that?" asked Tony.

"I do, Tony. If you provide a different software developer to Sagebrush at this point, we're going to have schedule slips. Our schedule is very aggressive, and our sponsor Leah Ranson will be irate if we don't get this new offering to the marketplace on time. If BSOD doesn't announce Sagebrush prior to the beginning of the fiscal year, a critical opportunity will be missed to capitalize on our client's need to spend fiscal year-end money."

"That's a tough spot you're in, Sean. But my hands are tied. My department manager has set my priorities and Sagebrush clearly falls below the CRM upgrade project on his priority list. I'm sorry, Sean, but Sagebrush just isn't that large of a priority in this department. I can't change my decision at this point. I need Shafik to work the CRM project. I'm assigning Randy Becker to Sagebrush. I'm sure he'll do well. He's got a lot of development experience."

Sean was stunned. He couldn't believe what he was hearing. He was well aware of Randy Becker's background
through discussions with Shafik. Randy was well-versed
in application development of web-based solutions using
scripting languages. But Sagebrush required an intimate
knowledge of object-oriented application development. If
Randy replaced Shafik on Sagebrush, he would not only
have to learn the software purpose and function, but also
be required to spend a significant amount of his time learning object-oriented programming techniques.

"Tony, that's totally unacceptable. I need someone with a
strong application development background. Randy Becker
is a web scripter, not an application developer."

"Sean, we need to grow the knowledge of our developers.
We need to do it on real-life projects like Sagebrush."

Sean stood up and headed for the door. "What you need
is to train them prior to assigning them to projects like
Sagebrush. I can't afford to provide training to a developer. It's not in the budget or the schedule. I obviously
need to follow up with your management. But thanks for
your time, Tony."

"I'm sorry you feel that way, Sean. But that's my decision."

Back in his office, Sean thought about what had occurred.
He had failed to make the case for keeping Shafik on the
project and may have also damaged his relationship with
Tony. If he were to get any project done, he'd need the support of the resource managers. As it was quickly approaching lunch, Sean decided to stroll to The Mud to see Mariah.

He was about to take her up on her offer of letting her know when he needed her advice.

Sean arrived at 11:15 a.m., just before the lunch crowd.

"Hi, Sean. I haven't seen you in here for lunch in some time," said Mariah.

"Mariah, I wish it were just for lunch. I need your help when you have a spare moment."

Remembering the discussion they had the previous evening, Mariah inquired, "Was this the day you were going to meet with Shafik's manager?"

"Yes. That's what I want to talk to you about."

"What happened?"

Sean fidgeted in his seat, "It was terrible. His manager, Tony, absolutely shot down my request to keep Shafik assigned to the Sagebrush project."

"What did he tell you?" she asked.

"He said that Shafik is needed to work on the CRM upgrade project, which has a higher priority in his department than Sagebrush. He then said he was providing me with Randy Becker. Randy's a great guy, but we need an application developer familiar with object-oriented methodologies. Randy is a web scripting guru, but knows very little about object-oriented application development. He'll simply expend my budget without having the skills required for Sagebrush."

"Did you explain this to Tony?"

"Yes I did. He explained that one of the reasons he was assigning Randy to the project was so he could learn object-oriented development. He's essentially using my budget to train his personnel."

As Sean explained his predicament, Mariah shifted in her seat and wondered what was really going on. Her instincts told her she wasn't aware of the whole story.

"I want you to recreate the scene in Tony's office. Tell me as exactly as you can how you asked him to keep Shafik on the Sagebrush project. How exactly did you open with him?" she asked.

"I told him that Shafik had explained to me that he was being reassigned to the CRM project and would not be available to work Sagebrush any further."

Mariah continued her questioning, "And then . . . ?"

"I explained to him that I needed to keep Shafik on the project to avoid schedule delays."

"And then . . . ?"

"After he told me that I was getting Randy Becker, I told him that Randy didn't have the skills I needed for the project."

Mariah sat back and thought for a moment. After a long silence, which seemed like an eternity to Sean, Mariah responded.

"Sean, I think I see what went wrong in the meeting. At what point did you ask Tony what he needed?"

"What *he* needed?" Sean asked, obviously surprised.

She responded in an equally a surprised voice, "You mean you *didn't* ask him what he needed?"

"No, I didn't. The purpose of the meeting was to get Shafik back on the Sagebrush project," said Sean.

Mariah asked, "And is he back on the project?"

"No. I think I'm beginning to see where you're going."

At that moment, it was as if Sean was struck with clarity and understanding. His shoulders slumped as his defensive posture gave way to understanding as Mariah continued.

"Sean, you spent the entire meeting discussing your needs and none of the meeting asking Tony what his needs were. You were basically negotiating from a single viewpoint— your own."

"So what should I have done?"

"Negotiation is something that takes much practice, Sean. We're often pretty lousy negotiators because we only see things from our point of view and don't pay much attention to the needs of the other party. When you fail to seek their view, you fail to build an understanding. If you cannot find out what they need, how can you expect to seek an intersection of your needs and their needs?"

Sean asked, "What do you suggest I do at this point?"

"Here's my suggestion. Go back to BSOD this afternoon and talk to Shafik. Discuss some of the issues and problems that are currently being worked on in his department, and by Tony. After you've done this, think about how you can help Tony with some of those problems. Do this today. You need to see him as soon as possible to avoid damaging the relationship any further. Open with an apology for putting your needs first and offer a solution that may help both of you find common ground."

Sean thought about what she'd said for a moment. He was not sure how to approach Tony after the meeting they'd just had.

"How can I best approach Tony, Mariah? I'm not quite sure what to say."

Mariah continued, "Try writing down the scenario first. Have you ever programmed, Sean?"

"Sure I have, Mariah. Why?"

"After you've got a few solutions or proposals for how you can help Tony, think of an IF-THEN-ELSE scenario. IF Tony states that the first suggested solution is unacceptable, THEN I'll propose a second solution; or ELSE, I'll ask for further clarification of what his needs are," she explained.

Doing this beforehand will help you gain confidence and you'll be less likely to be caught off guard when he responds."

"You've been right on the money before, Mariah. I see no reason to doubt you now. Thanks for your advice. I'll head back and try that now."

Sean grabbed a sandwich and a drink on his way out and was back in his office at 12:30. Most of BSOD was still at lunch when he returned. He left a voicemail for Shafik to call him when he returned from lunch. Sean began thinking about possible solutions to address some concerns that Tony might be facing. He thought about his project team and recalled that one of his friends in the IT department, Alan Davis, had previously worked at a company that provided CRM solutions to its clients. He called Alan to discuss his availability. As luck would have it, Alan was just finishing a server upgrade for the accounting department and would be available to work on other projects 75 percent of his time. He also discovered he had a keen interest in BSOD's CRM application. He was interested in eventually moving to the software development team.

Shafik returned to the office at 1:00 and returned Sean's call. During their discussion, Shafik had explained to Sean that one of Tony's major concerns was supporting the growing number of "high priority" projects with his current staff. It seemed every project manager that approached Tony had a project that was high priority. As Shafik explained, to Tony it was as if project managers were always pushing their own agendas and projects. Sean thanked Shafik for his help. Sean explained to him that he wasn't off the team just yet. He told Shafik that he should know by the end of the day if he'd made his case or not.

Sean called Tony to confirm his availability. After a bit of apprehension, Tony agreed to meet with Sean at 2:30. It was currently 2:00 and Sean had just enough time to take Mariah's advice to plan out some scenarios prior to their meeting. As the meeting approached, Sean made his way to Tony's office once again. He knocked on the door, and Tony invited him in. Sean sat in the same chair as he had that morning.

"Tony, let me first apologize for how I behaved this morning. I was self-centered and acted without any concern for your needs. Please accept my apology."

Tony looked surprised, "I can say with confidence that's never happened before. Apology accepted, Sean, thank you."

Sean continued, empathizing with Tony's issue, "Tony, it must be hard being a resource manager. BSOD is obviously stretched very thin on resources right now. You folks seem to work miracles by getting done what needs to be done with the staff shortage you have to deal with."

"You can say that again, Sean. I've been understaffed for about four months now. And as the corporate executives devise projects to grow the company, I only get stretched further," Tony said.

"I think I have something that may help both of us, Tony."

Tony looked intrigued, "What's that, Sean?"

"Well, Shafik's skills are critical to the Sagebrush project right now. If I lose him on the software portion of the project, we're sunk. It's hard to tell when the project could be finished—and for what cost. But I told you all of that this morning. I'm also aware of your immediate need for additional staff to help with the added project work being performed now. I happen to have a friend in the IT department who's been here for about eight months. He used to work for a leading supplier of CRM solutions as an application developer. His name is Alan Davis. I checked with Alan and his manager. He's available 75 percent to work on the CRM project. Alan's very interested in our custom CRM application. He also has the appropriate skill set to help you out and is interested in working in your department sometime in the future. You could consider this a trial period of a potential staff member."

Tony was stunned at Sean's offer and replied, "Now that's an offer I can't refuse, Sean. Consider it done. You have Shafik for the remainder of the Sagebrush project. Put me in touch with Alan. We'll get the ball rolling. Let me know if I can help you in the future. I've never had a project manager approach me apologetically and take my needs into consideration. Thank you, Sean. You're a class act."

Sean was ecstatic. He'd been able to turn around a seemingly lost negotiation by understanding and empathizing with the other party. Finding an intersection of needs allowed each of them to further their goals and drive to a win-win outcome.

CHAPTER 7

Multidirectional Relationship Management

" Friendship is a plant of slow growth and must undergo and withstand the shocks of adversity before it is entitled to the appellation."

George Washington

Project management requires a vast set of skills. Competencies such as scheduling, risk management, budget analysis, and procurement are all important to the successful completion of projects. But even mastering every technical skill won't ensure that you'll be a success as a project manager because, at its core, a project is completed by people. Think back to Chapter 1, where we discussed the art and the science of project management. The art involves working effectively with people.

Project managers need a hefty amount of people-savvy to deliver a successful project. Project managers need to build and grow relationships in every direction, including upward (to the boss and executives), downward (to project team members), and laterally (to colleagues and peers). Doing so will help you, as a project manager, continually expand your network. It will also increase the probability of your project success and your personal happiness and contentment. Refer to Figure 7-1 for a graphical depiction of multidirectional communication and relationship management.

FIGURE 7-1 The Art of Influence through Relationships in Project Management

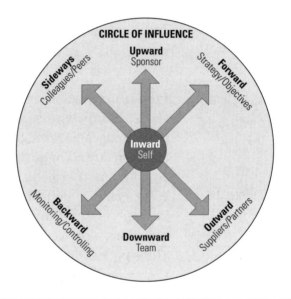

Throughout this chapter, these directional references will be used to differentiate individuals according to their relation to you on the organizational chart, not within the project team. In high-performing project teams, the roles within the team are viewed as existing on the same plane. (Surely, power differentials exist within a team, with each individual having a distinct and clear role with varying levels of authority and responsibility, but they should all be considered collaborative and complementary.)

When we're not at work, we're all on a general, professional plane—we're employed. When we arrive at the office, formal power structures unfold. All we need to do to understand this is examine any organization chart. There's a clear hierarchical structure. Some people are at the top of the organization, some are in the middle, and some are at the bottom. Project managers usually reside near the middle of the organizational chart. This being the case, we need to foster relationships in all directions, from the bottom to the executive level. A project manager's relationship and communication with team members, peers, his or her boss, and executives each represents a unique dynamic that must be successfully managed. More importantly, we must build rapport to enhance interpersonal relationships that will enable long-term friendships to grow and aid in the health and well-being of those around us as well as ourselves.

Lateral Relationships with Peers and Colleagues

In many organizations, project managers are in direct competition with one another. With the implementation of forced rankings, peer reviews, and competition for limited salary increases, why should project managers be motivated to build relationships with their peers? Because by doing so they expand personal networks,

TIP: Do not underestimate the impact positive relationships have on project success and in the workplace as a whole. By facilitating open collaboration and communication, you will be helping others succeed—one of the distinguishing features of an engaged leader.

improve work environments, and tap into a prime source of collaborative energy capable of pushing them to the next level of achievement.

Your peers share many of your struggles, and each has a unique way of coping with them—ways you may not have considered. Every time you reach out to someone new, you increase your potential, broaden your views, and enrich your experience—if you are open-minded. And by helping your peers win, you're really accelerating and winning with them. You'll build confidence and trust in one another, and increase your influence across the organization.

So how do you go about building those working relationships? First, you must understand your peers, what they're working on, and who they are as people. Offer your support and help even if they do not appear to need it; you'll feel better and they'll be more apt to help you when you're in need. The teamwork demonstrated by peers working as a cohesive unit can garner mutual respect, increase credibility, and bring increased influence.[1]

We must also realize when to let go of our ideas and accept better ones. As the strong-willed people that many of us are, we can occasionally hold onto ideas much longer than we should out of fear of giving in to competition. Fear is a selfish emotion because it protects us from something we do not want to face. When we hold onto our ideas too long, the fear of being seen as weak and unintelligent is the prime motivator. In actuality, by demonstrating the willingness to bend and adapt when better alternatives exist, we demonstrate courage, leadership, and collaboration.

Upward Relationships with Your Boss

If you had to choose your boss, would you choose the one you currently work for? If so, congratulations—you've achieved what the majority of employees have not. It's been said that employees don't leave their organization—they leave their boss. Why is it that so many individuals do not like working for their current boss? Is it because the boss lacks training? Could it be that the boss does not signal clear expectations? Is it a matter of miscommunication? Perhaps it's a combination of these and many other factors. By actively striving to know and understand the work of our direct bosses, we can begin to build meaningful relationships with them that can prove very rewarding, both professionally and personally.

> **TIP:** If you are a manager, it's impossible to overstress the importance of empathy and understanding. In today's competitive war for talent, being anything less could prove to be a critical organizational stumbling block. Put another way, if people don't like to work for you, they'll choose to work for someone else, be it inside your organization or for your competitor.

Effectively managing the relationship you have with your boss is critical to the success of you both. Doing so requires empathy and an understanding of your boss' role. Many project managers either do not understand, or simply underestimate, the amount of information their immediate supervisors need to do their job. They may likewise underestimate the amount of information and assistance they need from you. Do not assume your boss always knows how much (or what) information he or she needs from you. It's best to communicate too frequently until your boss tells you to slow the information inflow, than to communicate too infrequently.

Start by working to understand your boss. What does your boss need to do his or her job effectively? What type of information will be required and at what frequency and level of detail? Schedule a time to sit down with your boss to discuss these questions. While you may receive answers to the questions during the meeting, the process does not stop there. Over time, take note of how your boss responds to the information you're providing. You may have been told one thing in the meeting, but recognize different needs after you've provided data over some period of time.

TIP: After a period of time working with your boss, you'll begin to see how he or she operates, what information they require, and their preferred communication style. Try to identify these traits ahead of time and anticipate what will be required of you. If you haven't yet worked with this person, discuss this topic with your peers to help you gain an understanding of the boss' requirements.

It's important to understand your supervisor's pressures, goals, and concerns. Over time, you'll be able to identify his or her strengths and weaknesses. By leveraging your own skills to help your boss shore up some weaknesses and illuminate some strengths, you'll go far toward advancing the relationship dynamic with this individual who is key to your personal and project success.

Once you begin gaining a better understanding of your supervisor's traits, goals, and needs, you can begin to work on establishing a working relationship that has value for both of you. This relationship should be characterized by well-understood and well-communicated expectations, ingrained trust, and unambiguous goals.

Another strategy for building a healthy relationship with your boss is to make good use of their time and resources. Like all of us, your boss is a very busy person. He or she must accomplish numerous tasks each day and has scarce time to accomplish them. Ask your boss if there's anything you can do to help with her daily tasks. Doing so will also show that you're ready to take on more responsibility and could open doors that might previously have been closed to you.

Upward Relationships with Executives

Your boss is the person to whom you report most directly and with whom you have the most direct communication. But a project manager frequently also deals with individuals in the executive ranks. Project sponsors, for example, are typically at executive levels of an organization, and project managers typically have to report status to their project's sponsor. How you do this requires separate consideration because executives are very different individuals from direct managers or department heads, complete with different agendas and expectations. They need to be managed in a slightly different way than someone at a level just above your own, which is where your boss resides in the organizational hierarchy.

First, understand that executives have usually spent many years in an organization to attain the level they've achieved, and they usually have large egos—although this isn't universally true.[2] More importantly, they typically do not have the time nor the energy to stroke your ego. Therefore, focus communication and presentations with laser-like clarity to present relevant data. Executives are busy people who make numerous important decisions every day. Do not burden them with irrelevant data. Because they usually have very busy daily calendars, speak with intent and purpose to ensure you do not waste their time.

Do not expect specific directives from the executive ranks. Executives deal with large, high-stakes decisions on a daily basis. Once they've issued a broad directive, they take for granted that it's been dealt with by delegating it to you. If you ask for specific direction they may quickly deduce you're of less-than-stellar intelligence or capability. After you've received this broad directive, it's up to you to make things happen. You will not be allowed to go back at a later time to get clearer direction. Use your best judgment and drive results.

Finally, when dealing with executives, *never* tell them they cannot do something.[3] Unless you are dealing with an issue that is illegal, guess what? They *can*. Don't question their power or status. Typically, executives carry the clout to go around established process and policy if needed. If you have a concern, voice it with a clarifying statement or question. For example state, "I understand your point; however, have you considered . . . ?" A clarifying question or comment such as this acknowledges their power and will help move the situation forward.

Downward Relationships with the Project Team

When it comes to relationships with team members, I use "downward" only as a way of demonstrating the organizational, hierarchical position of the leader on the project team. The term is not meant to be interpreted that team members are somehow beneath their leaders. Your project team will have different priorities and agendas from you, and building relationships with them will require a slightly different approach than with other directional relationships. In that sense, your relationship to your team is not really downward.

I believe these relationships are the essence of successful project management. (We'll discuss the role of leadership in project politics and conflict in Chapter 8.) I firmly believe that having the ability to relate to your project team is the key to obtaining and sustaining long-term leadership effectiveness.

What is it that helps you foster meaningful working relationships with the members of your project team? There are a multitude of factors, but I believe one of the most powerful ways to build meaningful relationships is through practicing *authenticity of purpose.* Many books, seminars, and workshops discuss the importance of rewarding employees for their efforts and dedication to producing results. If this praise isn't authentic, however, it will be transparent. Put simply, you must relate to your teams authentically or they'll recognize the praise for what it is—insincere.

To successfully relate to your project team, you must empathize with their daily struggles. You cannot do this by spending all day behind your desk with your nose buried in email and schedules. Spend some time each day among your team. "Management by walking around," or MBWA, is a simple and effective way to demonstrate to your project team that you care about their day-to-day tasks and that their work is important to you. Most importantly, it demonstrates that you are engaged and present. Using this simple tactic also illustrates your willingness to listen to their concerns, which will go a long way in connecting with them.

There's a side benefit to MBWA that many often discount. If you spend all your time behind your desk, you may not get a clear picture of true project conditions when you receive reports. You'll be much closer to the true status and health of the project if you spend time in the working environment. Doing so offers you a great opportunity to witness and address potential issues before they become catastrophes.

Every one of us could do a better job at creating, building, and fostering relationships with our colleagues. We don't need to have group hugs at the office each day to do it. We will, and should, have disagreements and conflict. What relationship management is about is increasing our capacity to engage in these occasional conflicts and move through them and past them in constructive and healthy ways.

KEY POINTS

- Project management requires communication with virtually every level on the organizational chart, from front-line employees to corporate-level executives. Establishing and building relationships with persons at every organizational level is necessary to move the project toward a successful conclusion.

- Managing relationships with colleagues and peers is one of the easiest ways to stay "in-the-know." Building up favor banks with other project managers can provide an effective means of getting things done by cashing in these favors at opportune times.

- In general, keeping the boss informed of tactical issues will help build understanding and mutual trust, and serve as an opportunity to gather assistance and feedback. Work with your manager to understand each other's expectations, needs, and desires as they relate to your project.

- When working with executives, get to the point quickly, take sharp mental notes, and handle action items assigned to you quickly. Do not expect executives to give you crisp and clear direction; they expect those working with them to be quick and to have the ability to think and figure things out for themselves.

■ Be visible to your project team members. They need to understand that you're there to help them with issues as they arise. It is your job to keep them shielded from the bureaucracy so they can focus on the tasks at hand.

TAKE ACTION

■ *Record the names of the people you come in contact with during a typical day or week.* Note their personal work styles and how they interact with each other. At the end of each week, review these notes. The next time you interact with each person, recall their personal work style and try to adopt and match it as closely as possible.

■ *Understand your own personality, temperament, and work style* as a means to enhance your ability to work with others. Prior to working effectively with others, we must understand ourselves. An effective way to accomplish this is to take some type of self-assessment, like the Winslow Report mentioned at the end of Chapter 2.

■ *If you experience or witness a poor relationship within your team, engage the individuals and discuss the situation openly.* But remember that you cannot enhance a relationship if one is not yet built or if the existing relationship is damaged.

☐

Endnotes

1. John C. Maxwell, *The 360-Degree Leader: Developing Your Influence from Anywhere in the Organization* (Nashville: Thomas Nelson, Inc., 2005).
2. Marie G. McIntyre, Ph.D., *Secrets to Winning at Office Politics* (New York: St. Martin's Press, 2005).
3. Ibid.

Sean's World
The Mutiny Lesson

It was a fresh beginning to a new week. Sean arrived at The Mud at precisely six o'clock, as always. After several minutes of casual banter, Mariah opened her lesson.

"Tonight, we're going to discuss relationships," she said. "We should discuss how to effectively manage the relationships you have with others in the workplace around you. In an organization, you need to modify your behavior and your relationships differently according to where others are in the organization relative to your position."

"Should my behavior change depending on where the person is in relation to my position in the company? I try to treat everyone equally."

Mariah leaned back in the booth and explained, "You should treat everyone as equally and nicely as possible. But there's a difference in how you go about managing a relationship with someone you have to report to, someone who is your peer, someone who reports to you, and with executives."

"By the time I was in the middle of my career, Sean, I'd learned that we must interact and interface with those around us differently. How we interact is mostly determined by what our role in the relationship is, and what the situation deems necessary. I made some critical mistakes early on but, thankfully, I learned from them and adjusted my approach. Here's what I want to tell you first: everything is based on mutual trust. If trust isn't there, you've got to build it before you can even think about managing the relationship."

She smiled and continued, "I guess that's why wisdom comes with age, because sometimes we're so busy and get caught up in our daily activities that we fail to see what's really important—our relationships with others. They make everything so much easier."

Mariah continued, "There are two things in particular I'd like to discuss. The first is how to relate to your project team. The second is interfacing with executives. I had particular trouble with both of those lessons."

"Sounds good," Sean replied.

The expression on Mariah's face turned serious as she began, "Let's start by discussing your project team. The pendulum of relationships that I had with my project teams swung to both extremes. When I took my first role as a project leader, I was timid and passive. My project team sensed this and used it to their advantage. I would get overruled in meetings and let my team almost bully me around. Because of this, my first project failed and I took all the blame for it because I hadn't controlled my team."

Mariah took a deep sigh and looked toward the ceiling as if she were reliving her experience. "When I took on my next project, I overcompensated. I became the bully and ruled in an almost dictatorial fashion."

Sean inquired, "What happened, Mariah?"

"The same thing that happened on the H.M.S. Bounty in 1789. My crew—my team—held a mutiny. My reign as their project leader was overthrown and I lost my job."

"You were *fired?*" Sean asked.

"That's right, Sean. I was fired. It was both the low and high point of my career."

Sean looked surprised. "How could being fired be the high point of your career?"

"I learned some valuable lessons because of what happened. I vowed that from that point on, I was going to make every attempt necessary to understand people. I was determined to turn that negative into a positive. I decided to take some time and go back to school to learn a thing or two about people. I went to the University of Colorado and studied social psychology."

She continued, "My point is that I turned a negative experience into a positive outcome and learned how to work with my team so we could all reach common goals—the successful completion of my project and their personal growth. As you move forward in your career always remember to speak with authenticity of purpose."

Sean, obviously confused again, asked, "What's that, Mariah?"

"It's being clear and honest in all of your interactions with your project team. You must care about people, praise them, and enjoy being around them. The trick is that you can't fake it. You must be sincere—that's 'authenticity of purpose.' Be trustworthy, be honest, be firm when you need to be, and you'll quickly build the ability to relate to your project team. You'll have others wanting to work on your projects, which means that many of your resource problems will fade away. Honestly empathize with the struggles others face daily. Help them work through issues, both professionally and, on occasion, personally. Believe me, when you start to be seen as trustworthy, your team will bring all sorts of things to your attention. Finally, make yourself available to them. Show your face and be visible when they're actually struggling with their daily tasks. That will add to your credibility and character. These are all part of what makes 'authenticity of purpose' so effective. You'll become a better project manager and a better person because of it, Sean."

Sean asked, "That all sounds so simple and straight-forward. This should be common sense, shouldn't it?"

"Common sense isn't always common practice, you know," replied Mariah.

"You also wanted to discuss executives, Mariah?"

She replied, "When I was a project manager, I noticed that people would usually tread lightly around executives. Everyone was nervous about speaking the truth. They were afraid of making a 'career-limiting' move by speaking honestly and openly about real issues or asking for help out of fear of being perceived as incapable of handling problems themselves."

"I must admit, Mariah, that I fall into that category some-times myself," added Sean.

Mariah quickly replied, "If you can't speak the truth without fear of limiting your own career, you are not cut out to be a project leader—let alone a business leader someday. Show me a company with executive leadership that doesn't want to know the truth, and I'll show you a company I'd never want to work at."

"Is there something special about managing relationships and interfacing with executives, Mariah?"

"Executives are very intelligent people, Sean. Granted, there are exceptions to the rule, but they didn't get to the positions they're in by being stupid. They've worked hard to earn their positions—the ones that haven't usually aren't around very long. They have usually been through some pretty hard assignments and have gotten to their positions through a lot of personal sacrifice. They've got important jobs. They're busy individuals with a lot of responsibility to shoulder every day."

She continued, "If you can make allies of your executives, they are good people to have on your side. They've got a way of getting resources when you desperately need them and helping solve problems that are far beyond your power to solve."

Sean sat in The Mud for another hour or so as Mariah told tales of projects long since past and of her time in Boulder pursuing her degree. Mariah was fast becoming more than a mentor: She was also becoming a dear friend.

Devising a
Political Strategy

"A leader needs enough understanding to fashion an intelligent strategy."

John Kotter

Do you enjoy going to work every morning, ready to face the challenges that lie before you, or do you dread the thought of waking up and facing another day of back-stabbing, fighting, and scheming? If you go to the office with fervor, you probably have a political strategy. If you don't have a strategy, you're probably the unlucky benefactor of someone else's political game plan. Or you may simply have a naïve view of politics in general and refuse to take part. You cannot hold the title of project manager and avoid the political playing field. As we have stressed, politics is an integral part of organizational and project life. Do you have a political strategy to advance your project?

This chapter will look at some of the considerations of building a political strategy and how to best execute it. We'll look at politics and political strategy from an organizational standpoint, not necessarily from a project-specific viewpoint, because the two are so closely related.

There are several benefits to developing a political strategy.[1] It keeps you from wasting time on irrelevant distractions, and helps you work effectively with difficult people. It reduces personal stress and anxiety, and it can do so for the entire team. It helps build better working relationships by reducing the amount and severity of reactionary "firefights," and by helping you and your team become more proactive and forward-thinking. Clearly, achieving even just some of these objectives makes it well worth having an effective political strategy.

Observe and Plan

Developing a political strategy is much like managing a project. We start by assembling a plan, executing the plan, and making course corrections as situations and the environment deem necessary. But political strategizing has one added element—observation. To properly set the course, a project manager should observe the actions of others to further his or her understanding of their objectives and positions. Who has the power? Who really makes the decisions? (Remember that decisions are not always made by people at the top.) How is bad news received? How is good news received? The answers to these questions will provide insight into the political landscape of your project. Constant observation and awareness will be required to answer these questions.

Observation is not simply watching. True observation is interactive and ongoing. Pay attention to those individuals who always seem to be making the high-stakes decisions, and to those they interact with on a daily basis. Talk to these people to stay informed of important activities and to build power relationships. And assess your own ability to influence as you define your personal, political objective(s).

Discover Power and Influence

Personal power and influence can take many forms. First, there's formal power, which is usually related to an individual's position within the organization. For example, a senior vice president will have more formal power than an engineering manager. But that same engineering manager may have significant power as a result of professional and/or technical credibility, referred to as "expert power."

In both projects and organizations, significant influence is garnered by the trade of currencies—not just monetary currency, but anything valued by others, like information, for example. Information is very valuable in organizations. In fact, individuals may choose to withhold information to gain power over others who may need that information.

Who Really Runs Things Here?

I have witnessed several decisions that were influenced more with expert power than with formal power. I've seen engineers influence significant business decisions of upper-level executives because the engineers were well known in their field. Expert power is indeed a useful tool to possess.

When you are observing the political landscape, try to determine what currency people in the stakeholder community value. Information, advancement, prestige, or the need to be liked could be the major currency of interest. What is your currency? If the major currency is prestige, do you have some way of providing the prestige others seek?

Define Your Political Objective

Once you have a clear understanding of the project environment, you can begin to define your political objective. Essentially, a political objective is what you want to accomplish in a given situation. The political objective should stand to serve you, your project, and your organization. What are you trying to achieve by the implementation of this political strategy (plan)? What is the goal? Be as specific as you can. A good political objective may be to increase support for your project and increase your influence in the organization by enhancing interpersonal working relationships.

Assess Your Ability to Influence

To move your goal forward, who do you need to influence? Do you have the credibility, subject expertise, or formal power to realistically influence them? If not, who can you engage to help influence them? Do you have a working relationship with this person? Is it good? Being honest with yourself can help identify gaps that need to be bridged prior to moving toward your objective. Use the following list to help determine whether you have the ability to influence others as you move to advance your goals. The more truths, the higher your ability to influence.

	T	F
1. I have formal (positional) power.	☐	☐
2. I have identified the currency the other party considers valuable.	☐	☐
3. I have the currency the other party considers valuable.	☐	☐
4. I know others that have the currency the other party considers valuable, and I have the ability to obtain it from them for use to advance my goals.	☐	☐
5. I'm recognized as an expert in my field.	☐	☐
6. I have a positive relationship with the other party.	☐	☐
7. I understand the other party's goal(s) and I can help them achieve their goals.	☐	☐
8. I can count on certain allies to increase my ability to influence the other party.	☐	☐
9. I have powerful contacts the other party would value, and I'm willing to share these contacts.	☐	☐

Take Action

You have a political objective, have assessed your position relative to that objective, and have honestly assessed your ability to exert influence in the organization. You're now ready to begin implementing your strategy by building alliances, managing adversaries, and changing course as necessary—all to achieve your political objective.

Build Alliances

The fact that project management is about relationships cannot be overstated. The ability to connect with people and build networks relevant to personal, project, and organizational success is crucial. Without the ability to build healthy interpersonal working relationships, you are doomed to be a mechanical project manager—one who manages by schedule alone. Projects very rarely, if ever, fail for technical or mechanical reasons. They usually fail because of interpersonal difficulties, communication issues, and other people-related problems.

Discover who needs to be engaged to implement your political strategy and begin building a relationship with them if one does not already exist. By initiating a relationship and seeking help and direction from the individual, you'll often be building a relationship that may last much longer than your tenure at that particular organization. I have actually built some very sound relationships and networks at every organization I've worked for. I still keep in touch with many of the individuals to this day because I genuinely like them, not simply because they can advance my agenda.

The relationship-building process starts with you. It's not up to the other person to approach you to begin building a relationship—it's up to you. Take the time to discover what they're working on and offer to help. When building a relationship with a colleague, don't allow yourself to be the one who places things on someone else's plate—be the one who takes things off their plate. Ask them to identify the barriers that are currently in front of them. If you have the ability to remove some of the barriers, remove them.

Manage Adversaries

Playing the role of Michael Corleone in *The Godfather*, Al Pacino said, "Keep your friends close, but your enemies closer." We have to exist in the organizations we work for. This means that we need to work collaboratively with those around us, be they political friend or foe. It's not as easy as simply avoiding your political adversaries. In fact, we often have to work in close concert with them to keep the organization moving forward. For project managers, political opponents may include other project managers competing for much–needed, yet scarce resources. In other instances, our political opponents may include our own bosses. These adversaries are the ones standing between us and our goals and they must be managed.

First, assess the situation from the opponent's viewpoint. In most of the situations I've encountered, it's usually circumstances out of the opponent's control that are causing them to become an adversary to your goals. It could be that you are blocking the path to their goals, too. For instance, you could be holding a resource that is necessary to accomplish a specific task. Trying to see a situation through the eyes of others is the first step on the path to understanding their motives and actions.

Work to convert your adversary into an ally. Almost any situation provides a chance to do this. Consider why you're experiencing conflict, and remember that if you have to work together, you might have common goals and objectives at some level.[2] Try to find an intersection of common goals you both share and work from there. In most instances you'll discover that the commonality of goals is sufficient to reframe the situation into a win for both you and your adversary.

If not, you need to increase your political leverage. Do not engage in an outright power struggle. The cost of losing might damage your career. Rather, seek out other allies to help move you toward your goal. If you've worked to objectively see things from the adversary's viewpoint, you should have a good idea of their motives. Seek out allies that can help both of you achieve your goals. These allies should hold sufficient power and influence to get things done in the organization. Allies with limited or no power in these situations will do you little good.

Change Course as Necessary

As our environments evolve and our situations morph we may need to realize what's occurring and change our direction. It is very beneficial to understand when our current political strategy is not working, update our plan when appropriate, and have the ability to change course while still in motion. Is our political strategy harming our influence? Is it damaging our reputation? Are others being hurt because of our actions? Always be vigilant in finding the answers to these questions, to help stay focused on what needs to occur to continue down the road to your objective. Being flexible is a very important character trait to have at your disposal in project management. After all, the only constant thing about the profession is change. Be aware of how environments and situations change, and how you can adapt in those cases.

> **TIP:** Always reassess your position and ability to influence in light of current circumstances. Build alliances with powerful people in the organization, and keep in mind that these people may or may not have a high-ranking position in the organization. Always measure your position in relation to your target (goal) and make course corrections as necessary to ensure success.

Take Time to Reflect

Always allow yourself enough time to reflect on the results of strategy implementation. Always recheck your assumptions for accuracy. Have you used your time and energy wisely in the pursuit of your objectives? If your energy was spent on tasks or issues without any effect on your personal or political objectives, vow not to misuse your energy going forward. Consider whether you've had a positive impact on your project and your organization, and whether staying the present course will continue to allow you to do so. Finally, allow yourself the opportunity to appreciate your current status relative to where you've come from. Personal introspection is a healthy activity that allows you to reconnect with yourself.

KEY POINTS

■ There are a number of benefits to devising a political strategy. Having the confidence to know how to respond in any given situation is key to reducing stress and anxiety levels.

■ Develop a clear political objective to help guide you and your project when engaging stakeholders, constituents, allies, and adversaries. Devise a political objective for the project, whether for the entire lifecycle or for one meeting or engagement at a time. Be specific in your objective and refer to it often to maintain focus.

■ Always be aware of where you are relative to your objectives and goals. Continually assess the political environment to stay in tune with any strategy changes.

■ Understand how influence can be used to convert adversaries into allies. If you don't wield sufficient influence, garner support from other allies as needed. If you don't currently have allies with sufficient influence, work to build additional alliances and relationships with those who can help advance your project's goals.

■ Actively manage your opponents, measure your progress by assessing your position, and change course as necessary.

■ Take time to reflect on what you've accomplished and what needs to happen to further advance your political strategy. Investigate how you can make additional contributions to your organization.

TAKE ACTION

■ *Engage your political adversaries in discussion,* however uncomfortable, to turn them into allies. If you both have positive intentions, the meeting should be helpful and go a long way toward building a collaborative relationship. First, set the guidelines for the discussion and stick to them. Focus on discovering shared objectives. Next, share your point of view and try to actively listen to and understand theirs. Finally, seek ways to help each other reach personal goals, and define a relationship going forward.

■ *Carefully observe the interactions of the team members* during project team meetings, particularly if you have leadership team meetings. Undoubtedly there will be some who always speak up and others who sit quietly on the sidelines. Don't make the mistake of believing that those speaking have more power and influence than the others. Interview the team members to get a better understanding of their professional networks and how they relate to others. Individuals with a very large personal and professional network are often well-connected to what's going on in their environment, and are usually able to get things done quickly. Make note of who they are and talk to them frequently to help expand your network.

□

Endnotes

1. Marie G. McIntyre, Ph.D., *Secrets to Winning at Office Politics* (New York: St. Martin's Press, 2005).
2. Ibid.

Sean's World
The Review

It was now mid-June, two months prior to the Sagebrush announcement and launch. Development was nearing completion as the system testing phase was ramping up. There would be one more project review before starting the final phase of Sagebrush. This review in particular was an important milestone: It was the final gate that Sagebrush would have to pass through prior to the product announcement. Because Sagebrush was a strategic project, all major stakeholders, including BSOD's top executives, would attend the review. It was also a critical event for Sean, especially inside of BSOD. He would have CEO visibility and therefore wanted the review to go without a hitch.

The weekly meetings between Sean and Mariah continued. Over the past several months Sean had come to appreciate many things about the softer side of project management, and he'd put them into practice. Tonight, the two would discuss next week's final project review. Sean was eager to get Mariah's advice on how best to present the project review.

"Good evening, Sean," Mariah said in her welcoming voice.

Mariah and Sean both moved to the booth they'd become familiar with over the past several months.

"Are you ready for the project review, Sean?" she asked.

He responded confidently. "I believe so, Mariah. This is our last project checkpoint and everyone's worked so hard to get here. It would be a shame if the project were cancelled now."

Mariah looked up at Sean. "What makes you think it would be cancelled. If all has gone as planned, you should not have to worry about that, right?"

"That's true, but you never know," he added.

"Well, I guess you don't ever really know. But don't be skeptical, Sean. There should be no question in your mind whether the project is getting cancelled or not. You should have a strategy to manage the decision makers on the project committee that will be deciding on your project's fate," she explained.

She continued, "One of the best ways I've found to effectively manage the political environment surrounding my project is to devise a strategy that is focused on moving my project goals forward."

"That sounds great in theory, but how do you actually devise a strategy? Wouldn't it be largely subjective?" asked Sean.

Mariah replied, "I never said this was an exact science, Sean. Unfortunately there are no hard formulas for you to run data through. But I can explain the process that served me well during the latter part of my career—once I got smart about things."

Mariah explained, "The first thing you should understand is where you're going. You need to have a clear objective.

After you've got an understanding of the objective you're trying to realize, you've got to honestly assess your position relative to that objective and your ability to influence others to help you achieve it. After you've done this, you can usually see what needs to be done to move forward."

"What if I can't?"

Reaching for her cup Mariah replied, "Reassess and document everyone's position as best you can. I mean all the stakeholders. You have to identify your allies and adversaries. Once you know their positions, you can revisit your ability to influence. Occasionally, you may need to influence through others if you don't have the ability to do it directly. After you've done that, you may need to build alliances, and you'll most certainly need to manage your opponents. The last step in the process is to observe what's happening and change course if you have to."

"Mariah, how can I identify my adversaries?" he asked. "Sometimes it seems as though they're hidden in plain sight."

Mariah chuckled slightly as she responded, "That's often the case and something we need to be aware of. We need to assess everyone involved, Sean. Something that helped me was viewing the political situation from the perspective of others and paying special attention to the stake they had in the outcome. Since projects represent change, there's usually someone who's going to be negatively impacted by that change. Focus on finding those individuals or groups. That's where you'll usually find your most active political opposition."

This particular evening Mariah had to cut her lesson short. "Sean, my daughter Anne is flying in from Salt Lake City tonight and I have to pick her up at the airport. I'm afraid we'll have to cut short tonight."

"That's fine, I'll take your notes and read through them," said Sean.

Mariah got out of the booth and began to turn out the lights as she explained, "With your project review only two weeks away, you have to work quickly, Sean. I'd like you to go back to your apartment and come up with an objective you'd like to achieve for the outcome of the meeting. Write the objective down. Then begin studying your relationship with everyone who'll be at the meeting relative to Sagebrush. Try to identify your biggest proponents and adversaries. Next, examine your ability to influence each. Finally, try to devise a way to move the decision-makers toward your objective. Remember, you may need to leverage a relationship with a third party to influence a decision-maker indirectly. This is especially true if they hold the other person's credibility and reputation in higher regard than yours."

"Thanks, Mariah. That sounds like a challenging assignment. I think I'd better do it if I want to pass the project review."

"You're welcome, Sean. Good luck!" said Mariah, locking the door.

Later that evening Sean gathered his thoughts, along with pen and paper, and sat down at the kitchen table in his apartment. He did as Mariah had instructed. He thought about what he wanted out of the meeting and how that could be written as an objective statement. After much consideration and refining of ideas, he settled on what would be his objective. Sean's political objective would be *to gain majority acceptance of the Sagebrush project in the executive ranks and achieve authorization to proceed with Sagebrush.* His objective as he wrote it was focused on what he wanted to achieve from the project review. The project review would begin the home stretch of Sagebrush.

Sean then began to identify the people who would need to approve Sagebrush and who they might be influenced by. After viewing everything written on paper he had an easier time identifying what would need to occur to achieve project review approval.

Leah Ranson was obviously a very strong supporter of the Sagebrush project—she had been the mastermind behind the initial project concept. Sean knew that Leah was well-connected and respected within the executive ranks. Nonetheless, there was a problem. Some of the department heads were trying to influence their VPs that Sagebrush wouldn't be a good direction for the company to go in. But the VPs realized that several of the department heads were worried about losing their power bases— which would happen if Sagebrush were given the final green light. The department heads had been unsuccessful in having Sagebrush cancelled over the past several months. Sean knew they would be lobbying hard during their last chance to shoot holes in Sagebrush.

Over the ensuing week, Sean decided to test the old adage "the best defense is a good offense." He had his team pull together updated project status reports showing the positive progress that had been made on the project. They pulled together statistics on how quickly they were making informed decisions by effectively managing risk, how effective requirements gathering was allowing easier implementation, and how critical milestones had been achieved, allowing the team to realize excellent project execution.

Meanwhile, Sean scheduled a session with Leah Ranson to make sure the business case that was presented was airtight. The purpose was to defend the Sagebrush project by being proactive in reviewing the significant return-on-investment (ROI) that would be achieved through customer acceptance. He discovered that Leah had asked Lynn Williams to conduct customer marketing surveys over the past year describing the new product and services offered by the project. The surveys showed a high level of interest in the marketplace.

When the meeting day finally arrived, all this information was pulled together into a presentation communicating the progress made to date, the investment made by BSOD in the Sagebrush project to date, and the ROI business case showing the amount of time until break-even could be expected for BSOD, after which the company would begin realizing profits from Sagebrush.

The assault began almost immediately after the beginning of the meeting. As a result of their working session prior to the project review, Sean and Leah were able to anticipate virtually every tactic and issue raised. As a result, consensus was achieved and Sagebrush was given authorization to proceed to launch.

The Leadership Element

Throughout the book I've used the terms *project managers* and *project management*. In this chapter I will refer to *project leaders* and *project leadership*. I'm talking about the same people, but here I want to consider them in a different light—as leaders. This chapter is about the role leadership plays in project management—especially with regard to politics and conflict.

Chapter 7 began by explaining that hierarchical structures exist within every corporation, as illustrated in any organizational chart depicting the discrete levels of power positions within the organization. Regardless of your position on the organization chart, you can demonstrate leadership. Leadership is indifferent to position. Some of the best leaders I've known throughout my career and my life have been in the middle of their organizations. Some have been near the bottom.

A key trait of leadership is the ability to see when another individual has a better ability to lead based on the situation. Let's call this *situational leadership.* Many situations dictate that the current leader step out of the way and allow someone with skills better suited to a pressing problem to lead the team through a tough time. I once worked on a project team comprised of seven core team members. The leader was a very knowledgeable individual and by every measure a great project leader. However, when a key negotiation was at hand, this leader had the ability (and willingness) to understand that another team member was better equipped to negotiate our position. The outcome was a successful negotiation, a team that felt empowered and, ultimately, a greatly respected leader. Successful project leaders are aware of their own skill deficiencies and understand the importance of leveraging the team's expertise.

Traits of Effective Leadership

Numerous traits define especially effective project leaders and set them apart from ordinary leaders. Some of the more relevant leadership traits related to project management are the abilities to inspire others, to develop a motivating vision, to listen empathetically, to hold others accountable, and to communicate expectations clearly.

Inspiring Others to Follow

Have you ever had a leader for whom you'd do almost anything, and do it willingly? I've had only a few such leaders.

We often comply with the direction of those in formal positions of authority above us. But in many cases, this is passive compliance, not active following.

I spent four years in the United States Army. I was right out of high school at the time, and I had had little working experience; growing up in the Midwest, my only jobs were related to farming, which on most days does not involve a large team effort. Therefore, I was unaware of what constituted real leadership.

> **TIP:** Strive to follow your leader the way you'd want others to follow your lead. View your success and your leader's success as interdependent with those who follow you. Adapt to your leader's personal style of leadership. Recognize and complement his or her strengths and help shore up weaknesses.

Looking back on my days in the Army, I can now see that one of the most influential leaders in my life was a squad leader I worked for while stationed at Fort Riley, Kansas. I was a baby-faced kid just out of high school spending my days in the motor pool and practicing to be a combat engineer. My squad leader was a buck sergeant only about five or six years older than me, but he somehow possessed an innate ability to motivate us through his day-to-day actions more than higher ranking soldiers could.

How was it that this ordinary young man could inspire us so readily? One of his most noticeable traits was his ability to relate to us. As people move up in rank and status (military or civilian), they often forget their roots and their past. As they advance they shoulder increased responsibility and the pressure on them intensifies, taking them in new directions.

Our buck sergeant was available to his people, which is all too rare. He related to us on our level, yet he was firm when he needed to be. For example, he consistently pitched in and helped us with our work whenever he could. This created a deep-seated respect for him. As a result we were the most cohesive squad in our platoon. I'm convinced that, had war broken out during the time I served in his squad, I would've followed him willingly into a minefield or hail of gunfire.

Developing a Motivating Vision

Why exactly are we doing this project? What happens when we're done? What will I get out of my work on this project? These are some of the questions that project team members will ask themselves at the beginning of a project.

To become an effective project leader, you must develop a project vision and communicate that vision effectively to motivate your project team. I'm not talking about the vision posters you see in the hallways of many corporations. I'm talking about a vision that energizes, resonates, and inspires action in our proj-

What Are We Doing Here?

A leader who lacks a compelling vision is just as likely to damage morale as a leader who has no vision at all. For example, I witnessed a team of highly competent and motivated individuals flounder on what they thought were the correct tasks, only to find out afterwards that they were the wrong tasks. This cycle repeated itself several times because the leader had no idea where he was going. There was no vision and the team was unsure of what was required. Not surprisingly, a high turnover rate ensued, and the business unit was irreparably damaged.

ect teams. People want to be part of something larger than themselves. The project vision provides this setting and creates a bridge to cover the gap between what is and what will be. To help you develop a motivating vision, consider the following guidelines:

1. The vision should be in line with the goals and objectives of both the project and the organization. If one or the other is out of alignment, you may need to reconsider the project.

2. The vision should be challenging. A vision that is simplistic is either too near-term or is not well-conceived.   .

3. The vision should describe the end state. This provides a metric that will show when you've arrived at the goal.

4. Finally, do not forget the what's-in-it-for-me factor. Why would anyone *want* to work on this project anyway?

Listening Empathetically

To lead effectively, you need to connect with those you lead. Your team members must be able to approach you without fear of judgment or reprisal. When team members discuss issues with you, listen to them with an empathetic ear. Only if you are approachable and trustworthy will your team bring important issues to you openly and honestly.

On one particular project I was leading, a team member came to my office to discuss the project's status. Our schedule was very aggressive, and the stakes were high. He informed me that one

TIP: If you find yourself out of touch with what's happening on a daily basis, talk to your team members individually. Ask them to give you honest feedback about your approachability. If it turns out that you are not approachable in the eyes of your team, work to make yourself more approachable. By doing so, you'll find out about problems much sooner. Perhaps you'll even find out about potential problems before they occur.

of the deliverables would be late, causing the project to miss an upcoming milestone. Because I had established a level of trust, honesty, and approachability, the team member had been able to bring the issue to me while there was still time to correct the situation. In this case, I was able to speak to the customer and revise their expectations. As a result, the milestone was pushed back to an achievable deadline, which we then met. If I had previously reacted to bad news with directed anger or criticism of the team, this person would not have felt compelled or obligated to deliver the bad news. Of course, I would have found out, but probably not until it was too late to repair the damage.

As project leaders, the seeds we sow now will have a direct result on the results we reap later. Be mindful and caring when interacting with your team.

Holding Others—and Yourself—Accountable

To lead, you must be out in front where you can't hide behind anyone. Personal accountability is one the most genuine traits a project manager can display, and it will lead directly to positive results. Why? Because by holding yourself accountable for your actions you are doing two things: (1) you are leading by example and demonstrating the behavior you want your team to emulate; and (2) you are not blaming your team as an excuse for failure.

Recognize that as a project leader it is your job to do everything within your power, and many things outside of your power, to successfully *lead* the project to completion. Doing something outside of your power is what politics—in this context—is all about. In other words, it's about gaining credibility and influencing those who *are* in power to act on our behalf.

Exercising leadership and demonstrating personal accountability set an example. If you don't have personal accountability, you can't hold your project team accountable for their results, either. I've seen some great examples of personal accountability in action but, regrettably, several more in which project managers hid behind the team they were leading and deflected blame. One example of personal accountability occurred on a project whose output was an input deliverable to my own project. Without this deliverable, our project would be on a day-by-day slip. When the project manager visited my office to tell me the slip that was going to occur, he took responsibility by noting that he had failed to follow up with a problem vendor, which caused his project to have the delay. He also offered to travel to my customer's site with me to help explain the situation. His corrective action was to visit the vendor weekly and hold daily telephone calls with them to ensure they were taking the necessary action to resolve the issue. The result was that the vendor ultimately delivered only three weeks late when they likely would have slipped even further without remedial action.

Another way to foster accountability is to lead by example and to hold yourself personally accountable for results, ensuring that agreements are written and periodically reviewed. Project teams are very busy. Most of us work in a matrix environment and have responsibility to several projects and programs. By writing and reviewing actionable items, you increase the likelihood of having them completed. This is not rocket science, it is basic project management but, surprisingly, this review is forgotten in many instances—or simply not practiced.

Finally, if you have performance issues with the individuals assigned to your team, confront them and ask them what is causing their decreased performance. Simply asking the individual how they're doing can have important consequences, because it demonstrates you care for them as individuals and not simply as resources. We often avoid these instances for fear of confrontation, but do not let your fear deter forward movement. To lead is difficult, but do what needs to be done: If an individual's performance continues to be suboptimal, you may need to have the individual removed from the project team.

Here are some guidelines to help you develop accountability:

■ Clearly define roles and responsibilities.

■ Communicate goals, objectives, and expectations, and ask that interpretations be stated back to you to help ensure understanding.

■ Make sure only one person is ultimately responsible for each task.

■ If an individual consistently fails to complete their task(s), you may have to reassign that individual or remove them from the project team.

■ Communicate task priority and importance.

■ Follow up to ensure engagement and action.

Communicating Expectations Clearly

How can you expect the people you're leading to deliver what you're expecting if you can't communicate your expectations clearly? The ability to lead with clear direction is essential. Expectations should be unambiguous. The SMART acronym typically used for setting goals can be also used to test expectations—make sure your expectations are specific, measurable, achievable, realistic, and time-bound.

Expectations should be made very clear to your team, and they should be repeated often. Communicate your expectations visually by posting them on a project website. And state them out loud so team members can hear them. We often need to receive information in varied forms to fully understand and remember it.

Do not make the mistake of assuming your project team has all the answers and a complete encyclopedia of information of what needs to be done. The most effective project leaders will guide the process of progressively elaborating a project and will communicate their expectations to the team along the way.

Consider this example: You are a project manager new to an organization and have been assigned to lead the implementation of a new email system. The project team may know the minutiae of what needs to occur to complete the task of implementing the system. But the project team will need several items from you. You'll need to clearly communicate what you expect in return. For example, what is the time frame for completing the project? How large is the budget? How will you expect team communication to be handled? What are the

TIP: It is up to you to help the project team succeed. Project leaders will put in the extra effort to remove obstacles to the team's success. Removing your team's obstacles will keep your team moving in the right direction and will allow you to worry less about task completion.

milestones for deliverables? How will the team members interface with each other? Do not expect your team to know the answers without you telling them.

The DTAB Project Leadership Model

What management book would be complete without an acronym to guide us? Over the course of my career I've witnessed many great and poor leadership moments. I have always been fascinated by the subject of leadership and particularly how it plays out in the project management framework. As a result of this curiosity, I've assembled what I call the DTAB model of project leadership: demonstrate courage, think politically, act ethically, and be in front. I've witnessed leaders who demonstrate those four guiding principles deliver outstanding results in the project environment. Because leadership represents both action and behavior, each phrase contains both an action word and a practiced behavior.

Demonstrate Courage

To lead is to live dangerously.[1] Putting yourself on the line for other people and for a cause is not an easy task. Leadership in the project environment is especially dangerous. Because projects are temporary and unique endeavors, project leadership is about managing and leading through change. People do not typically like or appreciate change. As a change agent, you're disrupting comfortable ways of doing things, implementing new processes, and sometimes delivering bad news. As a project leader, you're serving as the one-stop shop of accountability to executive project sponsors with the power to do severe damage to your career—a very large responsibility to shoulder.

> **TIP:** For any leader, accepting credit for a job well done is the equivalent of holding a hot potato: When given praise, let go of it immediately and pass it along to the project team. Whether you hold on to it or pass it on, your team will remember you for it—count on it.

Think Politically

Companies have both a definable culture and an ever-changing atmosphere of competing agendas and complex interpersonal interactions. Successful project leaders think politically and successfully navigate a path from project initiation to project closure, delivering the project's objective.

Studies of leadership make one thing readily apparent—success is related to the amount of time leaders spend building, nurturing, and growing personal relationships. Project leadership is no different. When you think politically, there are three aspects to consider: interacting with those who support you, interacting with those who are against you, and interacting with those who are undecided and cautious. Spend a good amount of time trying to sway this last group of undecided persons toward your favor by building personal relationships and networks. Politically minded project managers work to forge effective relationships with everyone.[2]

Act Ethically

Most company mission statements make some mention of ethics. Yet employees may be left to wonder exactly what it means to act ethically. In project management, acting ethically means doing what is right for your project, your team, and your organization—without compromising someone else in the process.

The project environment is often filled with rapid change and uncertainty, two key ingredients that can lead to moral ambiguity.[3] When people face change and uncertainty, one of their tendencies is to protect themselves, which could include actions that are unethical. For example, if a project manager disengages from a project because he had a negative experience with the project sponsor in the past, project team morale might suffer as a result. Disengaging from a project without working to repair a damaged relationship with the sponsor is morally questionable.

When faced with ethical dilemmas, ask yourself if your reaction (or action) will impact the project, the team, or your organization. Ethics are essentially driven by attitude and belief. Great project leadership means acting in accordance with the standards set by your organization, communicating those standards to your project team, and ensuring they're followed.

Be In Front

Finally, you must be in front: Do not use your team as a shield to hide behind. You must be in front of them to lead by example, hold yourself and others accountable, and show your willingness to put yourself on the line for your team. Remember that if nobody is following you, you are simply not leading.

An insightful colleague once told me that one of the best crash courses on leadership is to lead an organization of volunteers. I've found this to be true. Volunteers do not need to follow you because of your position. Usually, they are there because they care about a cause or a project. However, if your leadership style does not fit with them individually or as a group they can easily leave. Become the leader that you would want to follow, and you will be well on your way to leading with a purpose.

KEY POINTS

- Effective leaders surround themselves with outstanding people and understand that they will not be the best choice to lead in every situation. Leadership is situational, and great leaders use the skills of their team members to the advantage of themselves, their team, their project, and their organization.

- Great project leaders inspire and motivate willing followers. The best leaders will be followed regardless of the formal authority they hold, simply because others have confidence in them, can relate to them as individuals, and believe in their vision.

- Great project leaders listen empathetically and are non-judgmental. The ability to listen with a caring ear is paramount to building trust. If you are empathetic and people can connect with you on a personal level, you'll find yourself with an endless stream of willing followers.

- Clearly setting and communicating expectations, coupled with the ability to hold people accountable for meeting those expectations, is another trait of great project leaders.

- The DTAB project leadership model is based on leaders demonstrating courage, thinking politically, acting ethically, and being in front.

TAKE ACTION

■ *Write down three occasions when you demonstrated courageous leadership.* Could you think of three? If so, what defined the situation? If not, why?

■ *Work with your team to develop a project vision.* Assemble the team in a room with a whiteboard and begin to outline a project vision. Ask questions like: Where do we want to be at the end of the project? What will the impact be when we complete the project? How can we affect the organization for the better by completing the project? Capture the ideas and discuss them in the group setting.

■ *Take part in a 360-degree feedback survey* to identify how others view you. This process can be quite eye-opening. Ask individuals you know will be objective and fair to participate. Also choose individuals from different organizational levels, like your manager, your manager's boss, your subordinates, and your peers.

□

Endnotes

1. Ronald A. Heifetz and Marty Linsky, *Leadership on the Line: Staying Alive Through the Dangers of Leading* (Boston: Harvard Business School Press, 2002).
2. Ibid.
3. Jeffrey K. Pinto, Ph.D., Peg Thomas, Jeffrey Trailer, Todd Palmer, and Michele Govekar, *Project Leadership: From Theory to Practice* (Newtown Square, PA: Project Management Institute, 1996).

Sean's World
Walking Outside Is Easy
When the Weather Is Good

There was a visibly excited and relieved gait to Sean's stride that must have been evident to all as he walked to Mariah's coffee shop. He had just passed one of the most critical checkpoints in the Sagebrush project. From this point forward he would have the ability to more easily attain resources, achieve credibility with his team, and gain exposure across the entire organization. The project now seemed to be on the fast track to launch. He knew he was at the wheel and that his foot was firmly planted on the accelerator.

"Good evening, Sean. You seem in an exceptionally good mood tonight. I assume the project review went well?" asked Mariah, noticing Sean's excitement.

"That's an understatement, Mariah. Leah and I met last week to devise a strategy to gain the authorization of the executive leadership team to move forward with Sagebrush. The meeting ran like a fine-tuned machine. For every attack or question we received, we had a response prepared and a counter that would alleviate the concern."

"That's great news, Sean! Congratulations."

"I owe it all to you, Mariah. Thank you for the help. Your guidance was more valuable than I could have ever imagined."

"Well, thanks, Sean. But you did the work, not me! Everything appears to be going your way now, Sean—beware and be ready."

He looked at Mariah with surprise. "What do you mean?"

"In project work, things always seem to come up at times when you least expect them. I almost always found this to be the case in my career. I can't tell you how many projects I've managed that had something occur at the most inopportune time. Whether a risk that hadn't been identified became a reality, funding sources evaporated, or a critical resource had a death in the family, something always seemed to come up. When things would get too easy I learned to put on my paranoia cap and search for anything that might cause trouble. Those difficult times are the ones that will define you."

Sean thought for a moment and asked, "Are you talking about leadership?"

"Yes I am, Sean. It has been said that it's easy to walk outside when the weather is good, but when it's storming, the same journey is much more difficult. So it is with leadership. Heck, anybody can lead when times are good. It's the difficult times that separate great leaders from the rest of the pack. This is especially true of project leaders. It's a hard job that becomes easier only with practice."

Mariah asked, "What type of a leader are you, Sean?"

"I'd like to think I'm a good leader," he said.

"The bottom line, Sean, is that it doesn't really matter what type of leader you *think* you are. That's because you are defined by your team, those you lead, and the environment through which you lead them. What I can tell you is that leadership is not a position. Leadership is about being in front and weathering the inevitable storms. To be a successful leader, your people must be able to relate to you."

Mariah continued. "As project managers, Sean, we sometimes overlook how important leadership is to us. Our job is to plan, execute, and close. By focusing so intently on these tasks we can sometimes lose sight of the larger picture. People don't necessarily commit to plans or tasks— they commit to a purpose and a cause. You simply cannot lose sight of that. Concentrate your efforts on leading the people through the process and create a compelling vision for the project that your team can grasp as the true meaning of the work they do on a daily basis. Create a compelling vision for the people to follow. Work from the basis of your own vision and get them involved so it becomes a shared vision. If they have ownership of the vision, they will commit to it."

Sean was very interested in Mariah's views on leadership, but the excitement of the day was beginning to really wear him down. He'd worked hard for the past two weeks in preparation for the review. He and Leah had worked several late nights putting together a strategy to get them past the meeting and into the next phase of the project. The next phase was just around the corner, and Sean would need to spend the next several days preparing the closeout documents of the design and development phase.

"Mariah, I'd better get going. I've got a lot of work to do and you've supplied me with much to read and think about. Thank you once again for your time."

"Any time, Sean. I'm sure you'll do great in absorbing the knowledge," she replied.

Sean opened the door and replied, "I'll do better than that, Mariah. I'll put the knowledge to practice."

CHAPTER 10

Implications

" **S** triving for success without hard work is like trying to harvest where you haven't planted. "

David Bly

After we recognize projects and organizations as inherently political in nature and accept that conflicts will arise, what are some other things we—as project managers—can do to become better leaders?

Create a Positive Project Culture

Organizations everywhere are full of individuals who struggle to engage with their work because of project cultures that don't align with their personalities. Each organization has a distinct culture that is strongly felt by the people within it. The way people carry themselves, how they interact, and their general attitude all help convey an organization's culture. As a project manager, you have the ability to influence and create a subculture for your project team. It takes a little time, but eventually you'll begin to see positive change taking place.

First, realize that people will not follow you unless they can also get along with you. Make yourself available to your people and you will benefit as a result. When communicating, remember to "be here now"—be diligent about staying focused on the matter at hand, preventing your mind from wandering.

Remember also that your team members are the individuals doing the work and that they're talented people capable of incredible things. If you treat them as people, and not just as resources, you and your project will be rewarded handsomely. Remember to use discipline to change behavior in the short term, and to use praise to change behavior over the long term.

Finally, remember that to create a positive project culture we must align our tasks to our people, and not necessarily the other way around. People find value in doing what they're good at and what they love. Not everyone is cut out for project work. But when people are doing what they love and are working for a purpose greater than themselves, they get excited about coming to work. They get excited about challenging and rewarding tasks.

Acknowledge the Existence of Politics and Conflict

We cannot confront conflict, nor can we effectively navigate project politics, if we deny they even exist. To acknowledge their existence and work within their confines is to embrace a golden opportunity to make a difference in the success of ourselves, our projects, and our organizations.

Do not allow fear, uncertainty, and doubt to cloud your ability to confront conflict or to make crucial and timely decisions. Rather, take action and respond in ways that are appropriate to given situations. Our attitudes are choices that determine our responses to issues—and our success.

Don't Forget Humor

In closing, I'd like to point out once again the sustaining value of humor. The ability to look at ourselves, our surroundings, and our situations with a sense of humor will go a long way to sustaining us in times of crisis. Never take yourself too seriously. Always try to find the positive in situations and do your best to laugh at the rest. The simple act of smiling at someone can help make their day.

Sean's World
Epilogue

Sean had assembled the project team at Mariah's Magnificent Mud. Sean felt that Mariah had been pivotal in the implementation of the Sagebrush project, and he wanted to share its success with her. They all watched as the announcement was made on the local Denver business channel. The official media announcement had been made at a press conference in New York City two days earlier. Sagebrush, now referred to as "BSOD Enhanced Business Services," had officially been born. The team's hard work had finally paid off. Now, time would be the ultimate test of the project's success.

Leah arrived late, because she'd just returned from the New York press announcement. She joined in the festivities without any prompting. Leah approached Mariah and shook her hand.

"So, you're Mariah?" she asked. "Sean speaks very highly of you."

"Yes I am, and thank you. Sean's a very bright young man. He's surely an asset at BSOD."

Leah replied, "I'm very proud of how Sean managed the project. He always seemed to have the pulse of the team and was able to divert negative attention during the project's development."

Mariah was very impressed at Leah's willingness to share her time and attention with the front-line workers. She was obviously aware of the source of the company's success.

"Leah, Sean speaks very highly of you also. He looks up to your leadership."

"Well, thank you Mariah. Leading is much easier when you've got great people. I've actually got a proposition for Sean."

Leah excused herself and pulled Sean aside to talk to him privately.

"Sean, I'd like to congratulate you on the outstanding job you did leading this project. The results were fantastic. The project was very well received in New York at the announcement."

"Thanks, Leah. I owe all the success to the team. This is truly a first-class team," he replied.

"Spoken like a true leader, Sean. And while it's true that they've worked together in the past, they have not been as successful or as willing to work together as they were when you were leading them," she explained.

Sean responded, "That's too kind, but I sure appreciate you saying it."

Leah shifted in the booth, placed her elbows on the table, and rested her chin on her hands, "Sean, you've done an outstanding job on this project. I've got a question to ask you. For some time now, BSOD has been thinking about assembling a project management office. The executive leadership board believes the time is now right to create the PMO. Would you be interested in heading the effort?"

Sean was stunned; he couldn't believe what he was hearing. He'd just completed the most challenging project of his career and he was now being asked to take the leadership role in developing and implementing the organization's PMO. His confidence wavered. He wasn't sure if he had what it would take.

Leah continued, "You'll have the resources at your disposal to make it a reality. The company is planning on spending five million dollars over the next 18 months on the effort. I'm in a tight spot, Sean. I need someone I can trust to lead this effort. You're the right choice for the position."

After a momentary pause Sean replied, "I guess you've found your PMO manager, Leah. Thank you so much!"

Leah responded, "Don't thank me, Sean. You earned it. But don't think it's going to be a cake-walk. You've got some serious work ahead of you. I chose you because I know you'll be able to deliver. Thank you, and good luck."

Later that evening, after everyone had left, Sean and Mariah were discussing the events of the past several months.

"Thanks for all your help, Mariah. How can I ever repay you?" he asked.

"Give to someone else what I've given you, Sean. Helping you has rewarded me so much, and I think it would reward you the same way. Remember, you've got a bright future ahead of you. Work hard, focus on your dreams, and always remember—never take yourself too seriously. Have fun with what you're doing, and make the most of it. Laugh whenever you can and enjoy life!"

Organizational Structures*

Because the power of a project manager is determined by the project's greater environment, it is important to understand various organizational structures. This appendix describes advantages and disadvantages of three organizational structures: functional, matrix, and projectized. The functional organization provides the least power to a project manager, and the projectized organization provides the most.

Functional Organizational Structure

This is the traditional business organizational structure and is sometimes referred to as the hierarchical organizational model. It is characterized by vertical lines of reporting and accountability. Figure A-1 illustrates the functional organizational structure.

Projects exist in hierarchical organizations as departmental projects. For example, the engineering department may develop a product that would then be transitioned into the manufacturing department. In this model, a cross-functional team comprised of members from

---

*This section is adapted from *Succeeding in Project-Driven Organizations: People, Processes, and Politics* by Joan Knutson (Copyright © 2001), and is reprinted with permission from John Wiley & Sons, Inc.

FIGURE A-1 Functional Organizational Structure

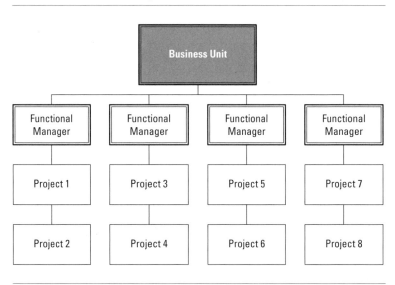

the sales, marketing, engineering, and manufacturing departments would not exist. Each of these departments exists with a predefined operational or supporting role within the organization.

The functional organizational structure provides the least amount of influence and power to the project manager. The project manager in this type of organization is typically a functional manager within a particular department who leads a team with a similar skill set. The attitude toward projects in the hierarchical structure is "build it and throw it over the wall." As work is completed in one department, the project essentially ends for that department unless problems that need reworking are discovered, in which case the project is sent back.

Advantages

▪ Requirements and scope are usually better understood with much less effort in a functional organization because the department itself usually generates the requirements, instead of gathering them from an external party or customer.

▪ Typically, communication is enhanced through team co-location.

▪ The learning curve is shorter because there are several subject matter experts within the functional team structure.

▪ Consensus and buy-in are more easily achieved because departments and groups with conflicting goals and interests are not involved.

▪ Project phase transitions are made with much less effort and forethought than in other types of organizational structures because deliverables aren't usually handed off to other departments.

Disadvantages

▪ It is more difficult to transform corporate strategy and direction into reality because a functional organization's link to actual project work is very weak if one exists at all.

▪ Reporting project status is rarely used as a means of executive awareness and decision-making.

▪ Informational silos (information existing only in one location) often exist between departments and groups in the performing organization.

- An organization can begin operating as a cluster of many smaller organizations, as opposed to one unified corporate entity.

- Quality control is often lacking because the quality functions are performed, if at all, by members of the project team who developed the product and thus have a biased view of product quality.

Matrix Organizational Structure

Today, the majority of projects are carried out in a matrix environment. The matrix structure enables the sharing of resources across functional units while maintaining a traditional hierarchical reporting structure. In some instances, resources may be pooled by skill type (e.g., system engineers, testers, developers). In other instances, they may be departmental groupings (e.g., marketing, engineering). This can be a double-edged sword for the project manager. On one hand, the project manager has people at his or her disposal across functional organizational boundaries. On the other, these people do not report directly to the project manager, which requires the project manager to have strong skills of influence and negotiation.

Project managers in a matrix organization request personnel resources from a resource manager who oversees schedules and the use of the company personnel. Figure A-2 illustrates the matrix organizational structure.

A project manager's power and influence are more apparent in a matrix structure than in a functional organization. Project managers are requesting resources from resource managers, so the project manager in effect becomes the internal customer for the resource manager.

FIGURE A-2 Matrix Organizational Structure

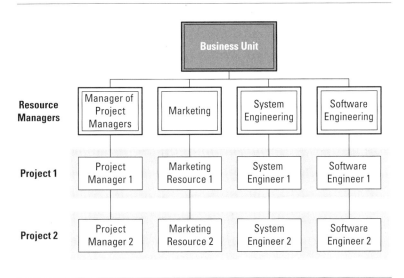

What often happens is that resource managers and project managers find themselves in conflict over whom the team member should take direction from. The employee is working on the project for the project manager, but the resource manager completes the performance reviews and awards raises to the employee. One way to help circumvent this issue is to negotiate with the resource manager to allow your input into the employee's performance review. This also allows you to gain leverage with the employee as a member of your project team.

Advantages

■ Changes in resource assignments are more easily achieved.

■ The leadership, technical, and management skills of functional managers are retained.

- It is the least costly structure for organizations performing major projects.

Disadvantages

- Defining and communicating policies takes increased effort and time.

- More time and increased coordination are required for handling complex issues.

- Resolving resource scheduling conflicts and priorities is more difficult.

- Increased communication interfaces increase reaction time to changes in policy, requirements, and so on.

- There is a greater potential for hierarchical competition and conflict between resource managers and project managers.

The *PMBOK® Guide* further differentiates the matrix organizational structure into weak matrix, balanced matrix, and strong matrix organizations. The weak matrix organization consists of team members from various functional areas, with no single person named as the project manager. This team is self-directed. The balanced matrix organization has a single person from one of the functional areas named as the project manager, who is then tasked with giving direction to all the other team members. Finally, the strong matrix organization has a centralized project management office (PMO) with organization-wide oversight responsibilities. In the strong matrix organization, the project manager may be a shared resource across the organization assigned by the PMO.

Projectized Organizational Structure

This is a pure project structure. In it, the team is assembled from across the organization on a full-time basis. The members of the team report to the project manager, not to a resource manager or a functional manager. Figure A-3 illustrates the pure projectized organizational structure.

From a project manager's perspective, this structure offers the most power. Essentially, in a pure project structure, the buck stops with the project manager. There are times throughout

FIGURE A-3 Projectized Organizational Structure

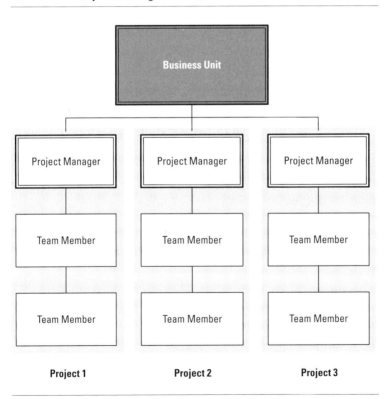

the project lifecycle, however, when team members may be idle or not have tasks that require their particular input. Additionally, when a project ceases, team members may feel apprehension about their next assignments.

Advantages

- Project teams are assembled quickly.

- Generally, management is kept well-informed on the status and progress of projects.

- Teams are usually more cohesive.

- Reaction time to changing conditions, shifts in direction, or priorities is reduced.

- Members of the project team typically enjoy high visibility with upper management due to the status of their projects. (Companies that are fully project-driven and otherwise projectized are typically less hierarchical.)

Disadvantages

- Functional organizations may resent the territorial encroachment of a special group that cuts across boundaries.

- Team members may feel apprehension near the end of a project because they may not know where they'll be assigned next.

- Any urgency of effort as milestones and deadlines approach may lead to overloading the group.

■ Leading a very large and complex project may prove cumbersome and unwieldy for a single project manager handling it alone.

The construction industry has traditionally used a pure projectized structure. In the typical construction environment, the project manager is responsible for assembling a team of core members, subcontractors, and laborers. Every aspect of the project is under the project manager's direct control, and team members do not report to functional managers. At the end of the construction project, usually the entire team is moved to another project.

Political Savvy Quiz Answers*

The quiz is a learning tool designed to elicit your preconceived ideas about political savvy. It's not a pass or fail test, so don't get too drawn into your score. Instead, focus more on the explanations—they offer more to learn than your score. As you will see, many of statements in the quiz should be considered false.

Politically Savvy Individuals . . .

1. *Politically savvy individuals sometimes have to manipulate the situation to get results.*

False. Some people view manipulation as a neutral word and feel like everyone "manipulates" to some degree. Yet, most secondary definitions suggest the term means using others in a negative way. Research indicates that most politically savvy individuals avoid even using the word *manipulation,* because it is too often associated with unethical behavior. Savvy project managers make sure their actions are ethical and avoid manipulating people.

---

*This section is adapted from *Quiz: Political Savvy Responses vs. Your Responses,* by Joel R. DeLuca, Ph.D., http://www.political-savvy.com/docs/results.asp (accessed March 29, 2007). Reprinted with permission from Evergreen Business Group (Copyright © 2007).

2. *Politically savvy individuals recognize that dealing with organizational politics is a necessary evil.*

False. Some politically savvy individuals see politics as a necessary burden that someone inevitably has to participate in. However, most savvy project managers look for win-win situations. A win-win approach to organizational politics actually provides a source of zest and a positive sense of contribution, not just a necessary evil. Working this way is generally associated with an effective leadership style, especially when working with the variety of stakeholders in any given project.

3. *Politically savvy individuals generally exhibit superior interpersonal skills.*

False. Amazingly enough, those seen as savvy by their colleagues don't score significantly higher on interpersonal-skill measures than their non-savvy counterparts. The difference has more to do with their strategic mindset and their savvy tactics. This is not to say that interpersonal skills aren't valuable—of course they are—but they were not perceived as the key to being politically savvy. In practice, interpersonal skills work hand in glove with political-savvy skills, strategies, and tactics.

4. *Politically savvy individuals are often more likely to work alone.*

False. The savvy know they need to build coalitions and strong interpersonal relationships to make an impact.

5. *Politically savvy individuals generally care a lot about ideas.*

True. Absolutely! Ideas allow the savvy to be inspired by something greater than themselves. Working with ideas for the greater good of the business enables them to play fairly with others.

6. *Politically savvy individuals are as likely to take credit as give it.*

False. The wording here is a little tricky, since people generally give about as much credit as they get (and unfortunately, that's not very much). However, most savvy project managers give far more credit than they receive. Like great winning coaches and players, they credit others more than themselves, knowing that well-spoken credit is often conducive to the greater success of the whole team. Giving credit where due is one of the key distinctions between the savvy and those who put their own self-interests first.

7. *Politically savvy individuals often take significant risks to attain important goals.*

False. The savvy, much to the surprise of many, do not generally take significant risks. Instead, they are excellent at managing risk to reduce it, just as effective entrepreneurs often do. They do take smart risks, though, increasing their odds of success and influence more than those who avoid risk altogether.

8. *Politically savvy individuals invest a great deal in making decisions more rational.*

True. This is one of the ironies of the savvy individual. Many rationalists, who are technically expert but relatively passive when it comes to organizational influence, believe that business decisions should be rational. Often, however, the result of these purely rational decisions is just the opposite of what's intended because they haven't considered and factored in the impact of negative politics. Savvy individuals use a broader understanding of human nature, which acknowledges people as only partly—not entirely—rational. As a result of this acknowledgment, savvy individuals work hard to prevent dysfunctional politics from driving decisions, and they are actually able to achieve rational results more than those who don't acknowledge human nature.

9. *Politically savvy individuals are willing to confront those they know are acting purely out of self-interest.*

False. Confronting a skilled Machiavellian often backfires, and you will be perceived as jealous or foolish. Allowing the self-interested to trip themselves up is likely a more effective approach.

The Results

1–3 Matches

Scores at this level are generally not due to a lack of innate intelligence; very intelligent individuals can score this low. More likely, the level represents a mindset that is traditionally hierarchical, command-and-control in nature, and believes in being completely straightforward. This mindset is understandable given the significant number of organizations that foster this kind of culture.

4–5 Matches

This is the most frequent range of scores. It often represents the traditional view of political savvy. People in this range generally see the world as less black-and-white than those scoring at the 1–3 level of matches. Attaining this level puts one with most other intelligent individuals who work within the traditional views of hierarchical organizations, but who also recognize that the human dimension plays a significant role in organizations.

6–7 Matches

This level of matches often represents those who are likely to be as conscious of the informal organization as they are of the formal organization. Astute awareness of both enables them to use both formal and informal approaches to influence others. Consequently, they are likely to be more successful at getting things accomplished.

8–9 Matches

This level most likely includes people who are naturally politically savvy. They probably have intuitively integrated human nature and hierarchical expectations within an ethical framework. The issue here is to ensure that such integration moves from something intuitive and implicit to something conscious and explicit, so these individuals can better lead, coach, and develop others as they apply their full range of politically savvy tools. Congratulations! Only about 5 percent achieve this level of matches.

Index

A
accountability, 172–174
acknowledging politics and
    conflict, 186–187
active listening, 100–101,
    117–118
adversaries, managing, 156–157
alliances, 155–156
art of influence, 133–135
art of project management, 2
authenticity of purpose, 141
authority, 7, 12

B
balanced matrix organization
    structure, 198
barriers to communication,
    93–94
beginning phase, project lifecycle,
    27–28
blame, 172
boss, relationship with,
    137–139

C
challenges, project environment
    communication, 3–4
    competition for scarce resources,
    4–5
    key points, 12
    lack of power, 6–8
    project globalization, 8–11
    taking action, 12–13
    unclear project goals, 5–6
change, 34
closing process, 51–52
colleagues, relationship with,
    135–136
communication
    active listening, 100–101
    barriers to, 93–94
    cultural differences, 96–97
    importance of, 3–4, 12
    interpersonal style differences,
    95–96
    interpretation, 94–95
    key points, 102

modes, 90–91
perception and physiological
  response awareness, 97–99
personal filter awareness,
  99–100
project environment challenges,
  3–4
skill, 89–90
taking action, 102–103
verbal, 91
visual, 91–93
written, 93
competition for scarce resources,
  4–5, 49
conflict
  accommodating, 56
  avoiding, 56
  closing process, 51–52
  collaborating, 56–57
  competing, 55
  competing for scarce resources,
    49
  compromising, 57
  constructive conflict, 52–53
  destructive conflict, 54
  executing and controlling
    processes, 50–51
  generational differences,
    57–59
  initiating process, 48–49
  key points, 59–60
  knowing your team, 49
  necessity of, 46–47
  planning process, 50
  proactively managing, 45
  process groups, 47–48
  reducing ambiguity, 48–49
  resolution modes, 54–57
  taking action, 60
  types, 52–54
constructive conflict, 52–53

courage, 176–177
cultural differences, impact on
  communication, 96–97

D
decisions, 205–206
deliverables, stakeholder influence,
  69–70
destructive conflict, 54
downward relationships, 2–3,
  140–142
DTAB model, 176–179

E
emotions and conflict, in negotiation, 118–120
ending phase, project lifecycle,
  29–30
ethics, 177–178
executing and controlling
  processes, 50–51
executives, relationship with,
  139–140
expectations, 175–176
external stakeholders, 72

F
functional manager, 7
functional organization structure
  advantages, 195
  definition, 7
  diagram, 194
  disadvantages, 195–196
  hierarchical, 193–194
  project manager influence,
    194

G
generational differences,
  57–59
goals, defining, 5–6

H
hierarchical organization. *See* functional organization structure
humor, 187

I
ideas, importance of, 204
identifying stakeholders, 71–72
influence
    art of, 2–3, 133–135
    assessing ability to, 154–155
    stakeholders, 75–76
information technology (IT), 4
initiating process, 48–49
inspiring others to follow,
    168–170
interest, of stakeholders, 73–74
internal stakeholders, 72
interpersonal skills, 204
interpersonal style differences,
    95–96
interpretation, impact on communication, 94–95
IT. *See* information technology

K
knowing your team, 49

L
lateral relationships, 2–3, 135–136
leadership
    accountability, 172–174
    acting ethically, 177–178
    being in front, 178–179
    communicating expectations
        clearly, 175–176
    demonstrating courage, 176–177
    developing a motivating vision,
        170–171
    DTAB model, 176–179
    effective, 168

importance of, 167–168
inspiring others to follow,
    168–170
key points, 179
listening empathetically,
    171–172
situational, 168
taking action, 180
thinking politically, 177
leading by example, 172
lessons learned, 11–12
listening empathetically, 171–172

M
management by walking around
    (MBWA), 141
manipulation, 203
mapping stakeholders, 78–80
matrix organization structure
    advantages, 197–198
    balanced matrix, 198
    definition, 7, 196
    diagram, 197
    disadvantages, 198
    project manager influence,
        196–197
    strong matrix, 198
    weak matrix, 198
MBWA. *See* management by walking around
middle phase, project lifecycle,
    28–29
modes of communication, 90–91
multidirectional relationship
    management
    art of influence, 133–135
    downward relationships, 2–3,
        140–142
    key points, 142–143
    lateral relationships, 2–3,
        135–136

taking action, 143
upward relationships, 2–3,
137–140

N
negative politics, 23–24
negotiation
active listening, 117–118
considerations, 114–115
emotions and conflict, 118–120
importance of, 111–112
key points, 120–121
need for, 112–114
preparing for, 115–117
taking action, 121–122

O
organizational culture
change, 34
organizational dynamics, 32–34
politics, 30–31
pros and cons, 31–32
organizational dynamics, 32–34
organizational politics, 204
organizational structures, 7

P
peers, relationship with, 135–136
perception and physiological
response awareness, 97–99
personal filter awareness, 99–100
planning process, 50
PMI. *See* Project Management
Institute
PMO. *See* project management
office
political objectives, defining,
154
political savvy
importance of, 5
quiz, 24–25, 203–207

political strategy
assessing the ability to influence,
154–155
building alliances, 155–156
changing course, 158
defining political objectives, 154
discovering power and influence,
153–154
importance of, 151–152
key points, 159
managing adversaries,
156–157
observing and planning,
152–153
taking action, 160
taking time to reflect, 158–159
politically savvy quiz, 24–25,
203–207
politics
importance of understanding,
21–22
key points, 36–37
negative, 23–24
organizational, 22–23
organizational culture,
30–34
positive, 23
project lifecycle, 25–30
project management, 24–25
self-awareness, 34–36
taking action, 37
positive politics, 23
power and influence, discovering,
153–154
project characteristics, 1–2
project culture, 185–186
project environment
challenges, 3
characteristics of, 1–3
project globalization, 8–11
project leader, 167

project lifecycle
  beginning phase, 27–28
  ending phase, 29–30
  middle phase, 28–29
  politics, 25–26
Project Management Institute
  (PMI), 5, 69
project management office (PMO),
  198
project management, art and science of, 2
project team members, relationship with, 140–142
projectized organization structure
  advantages, 200
  definition, 7, 199
  diagram, 199
  disadvantages, 200–201
  project manager influence,
    199–200
proximity, of stakeholders, 74–75

R
reducing ambiguity, 48–49
risk, 205

S
science of project management, 2
self-interest, 206
situational leadership, 168
stakeholders
  analyzing interest, 73–74
  assessing influence, 75–76
  definition, 69–70
  determining proximity, 74–75
  developing strategies, 76

external, 72
identifying, 71–72
information gathering, 72–73
internal, 72
key points, 80
management process overview,
  70–71
mapping, 78–80
predicting behavior, 76–77
striking balance, 77–78
taking action, 80–81
strength, weakness, opportunity,
  and threat analysis (SWOT),
  75–76
strong matrix organization structure, 198

T
taking credit, 205
The *Stakeholder Circle™*, 78, 80

U
unclear project goals, 5–6
upward relationships, 2–3,
  137–140

V
verbal communication, 91
vision, 170–171
visual communication, 91–93

W
weak matrix organization structure,
  198
working alone, 204
written communication, 93